It Works for Me: Becoming a Publishing Scholar/Researcher

Shared Tips for the Classroom Professional

Hal Blythe
Foundation Professor of English
Eastern Kentucky University

Charlie Sweet
Foundation Professor of English
Eastern Kentucky University

NEW FORUMS
Stillwater, Oklahoma
U.S.A.

NEW FORUMS PRESS INC.

Published in the United States of America
by New Forums Press, Inc.
1018 S. Lewis St.
Stillwater, OK 74074
www.newforums.com

Copyright © 2010 by New Forums Press, Inc.

All rights reserved. No part of this publication may be reproduced or transmitted in any form or by any means, electronic or mechanical, including photocopy, or any information storage or retrieval system, without permission in writing from the publisher.

Library of Congress Cataloging-in-Publication Data Pending

This book may be ordered in bulk quantities at discount from New Forums Press, Inc., P.O. Box 876, Stillwater, OK 74076 [Federal I.D. No. 73 1123239]. Printed in the United States of America.

ISBN 10: 1-58107-200-7
ISBN 13: 978-1-581072-00-6

Other Titles in the Series
It Works for Me!
It Works for Me, Too!
It Works for Us, Collaboratively!
It Works for Me, Online!
It Works for Me as a Scholar-Teacher!

Table of Contents

Foreword v

Introduction ix

Developing a Scholarly Frame of Mind 1

Creating Your Scholarly Plan 3

Overviews 11
    Getting Published: Inquiring Minds Want to Know 11
    The Not-So-Obvious Strategies to Become a Publishing Research Scholar 14
    Tips for Being Published in Academic Journals 16
    Academic Publishing from an Unknown Regional University 18
    Maintaining Scholarship in a Teaching-Focused Institution 21
    Dave's Hints for Publishing 23
    My Story 24
    When Life Intervenes 25
    A Transitional Journey 28
    Order with Flexibility 30

Pre-Writing 33
    Working with the IR Office 33
    Identifying Emerging Topics of Scholarly Interest in the Discipline 35
    Differentiating Journals 37
    How to Get Involved in Research 39
    Getting Started in Scholarly Writing 41
    Writing Book Chapters for Publication 42
    Time: The Elusive Ingredient in a Successful Recipe 44
    When You Really Need It Published 47

Writing 51
    Free to Write: Capturing the Creative Flow 51
    A Research/Scholarly Paper Outline 52

    A Timely Trifecta 54
    Getting Down to the Real Work of Scholarly Writing 56

Post-Writing 59
    For Improved Scholarship, Know Your Editor(s) 59
    Submitting a Manuscript? Do the Homework! 60
    Applying Wagnerian Opera Theory to Scholarship: It's Not over Till 62
    Turning Rejection Letters into Positive Advice 64

Other Scholarly Matters 67
    Collabowriting Your Scholarship 67
    Listen and Learn 73
    Five Strategies for Successful Co-Authoring of Articles 75
    Virtual Collaboration 77
    An International Learning Community: Successful Vehicle for Scholarship 79
    The ABCs of Writing Groups at Small Universities 79
    A Writing and Publication Group Becomes an Intellectual Community 83
    Stalking the Reluctant Professor: How to Find a
        Mentor without Getting Arrested 87
    Why Is It So Darned Hard to Get that Article Pushed out the Door? 89
    Collaboration Is King: Five Tips for Publishing Research Papers 91
    Using Authentic Data in Classroom Exercises 93
    A Scholarly Assignment 94
    Co-Creating with Students: Establishing Trust in a
        Student-Faculty Research Group 95
    Getting Published as a Graduate Student 97
    Checking the Checker 99

New Directions 101
    New Directions in Scholarship 101
    Creating SOTL: An Experiment in Collaboration 104
    Blending Service into Scholarship 108
    Publishing Ideas from Courses that Extend
        Beyond Your Primary Discipline 111
    S-t-r-e-t-c-h-i-n-g Yourself: Writing Outside Your Comfort Zone 113
    Young Adult Literature as a Publishing
        Venue for the Higher Education Scholar 113
    Sustaining Scholarship in a Digital Era 117
    Presenting Live in South Africa ... from My Family Room 119
    Merging Discipline-Based Scholarship with the Scholarship of Teaching 121

Foreword

Four decades of writing and giving workshops to help others write have convinced me that ninety-nine percent of the people I've met can take their scholarship to the next level if they are willing to work. Each time a scholar decides to go for it, this decision opens a door to a new and exciting world. Mysteriously, this commitment also turns would-be work into play.

Writers are generous people, who love to share. That's why they write. Well, that's one reason they write. Scholars know that writing improves their thinking and enriches their scholarship. Writing is often described as a lonely act. Perhaps that's true for those who never fully commit themselves to serious writing. But those who do commit to become the best they can be find that writing takes them to a private world, a world which, for really serious writers, is everything but lonely. On the contrary, it is most stimulating and enjoyable.

Seldom do readers have an opportunity to see inside the worlds of other writers. This makes *It Works for Me: Becoming a Publishing Scholar/Researcher* very special. The contributors to this book are inviting us to visit their private worlds. Before you begin exploring their worlds, think about your own world of scholarship, and sort out the topics that you find the most exciting. This reflection will prepare you to do more than visit these other worlds; once inside each world, you want to immediately look around and take something back with you. Knowing your passions in advance will enable you to capture those ideas that connect to your own world.

Welcome to My World

I hope you enjoy time travel. If so, let's go backward for about four centuries to the year 1619. Our new world is being born; Jamestown Colony is about 10 years old and Plymouth Colony is just starting. Over in France, a 23-year old Frenchman name Rene Descartes has just finished college, and on October 10 of this same year he realizes that he knows almost nothing. The only two things he really knows for sure are: (1) that he exists ("I think, therefore I am") and (2) that everything in the universe is connected. In this same year, the great astronomer Johannes Kepler is now 50 years old. He has verified Copernicus's heliocentric theory, putting Ptolemy's 1400 year-old geocentric theory to rest. Kepler, like many of his colleagues, saw such strong connections and harmony among the planets that he believed that the planets are connected, not only to each other but also to men's souls, an idea called "the music of the spheres." Throughout his life, Kepler pursued this idea.

In his 1996 inaugural address, Nelson Mandela advised us to share our successes, empowering and freeing others to share theirs. In my writing workshops, I follow this advice, telling my audiences that over the past four decades I have averaged a book and about eight national, refereed articles a year, and that I write each 70-page book chapter in a single sitting. I want them to know that if I can do it, anyone can. When asked how I manage that, I have my answer ready: "By going into my writing world and making connections." Just like time travel, you have to enter a small space and close the door, making your small world soundproof. Here, I can write easily and fluidly, whether I am sitting quietly at home or in the busiest airports and the noisiest food courts.

At this point, someone wants to know how I can close that door so tight that it isolates me from the outside world? I have two answers. First, I write about topics that I find "spellbinding." Second, I study my brain. My brain (maybe not yours, but mine) works like a diesel engine. It stays in a sluggish mode most of the time and has to have time to warm up. Then, when it does get going, the hotter it gets, the better it runs. That's why I write in 3 to 4-hour blocks.

My brain isn't very original. I'm not complaining, apologizing, or trying to appear modest, just analytical. I get most of my ideas from others. To illustrate how unoriginal my brain really is, unlike most people I know, I find ordering at fast-food restaurants a real challenge, and ordering for two or more impossible. That alone tells me that my brain is sluggish. So, I avoid drive-throughs and multiple orders. Even the idea of studying my brain and my behavior isn't original. I borrowed this idea from Benjamin Franklin, who ended each day by evaluating his day's work, using a written self-evaluation scale that he developed for this purpose. Third, I borrowed a habit from Isaac Newton. When asked why he was able to see the universe so much clearer than anyone else, he said he thought it was because he held each idea in his brain for longer periods of time than other people do. Translation: "Don't write until you have something to say." I don't mean to be coy. For 25 years my biennial survey to editors has found this tendency to be the second largest mistake that leads to rejections. I resist the urge to begin writing an article or chapter until I have thought it through completely. When I write with my hand, I am only copying that which has already been written in my mind. In his little book *The Prophet,* Kahlil Gibran wrote, "The wise man does not bid you enter his house of wisdom but leads you to the threshold of your own mind." So I'm not suggesting that you share my mental limitations or that my strategy would work for you. But I am suggesting that you reflect on your own thinking, and then develop habits that work well for you.

This book is wonderfully practical. Seldom do we get the opportunity to observe the working habits of others. But here, the many scholars who have contributed tips are inviting us to join their worlds of scholarship. As you enter each of these private worlds, remember that all things are connected. So, enter each professor's world with a purpose; immediately look around and see what you can borrow that connects to your world.

Second, if you are not using Text and Academic Authors Association (TAA), check it out on www.taaonline.net. This is a nonprofit association whose purpose is to help scholars in all disciplines improve their writing. Through on-site workshops, teleconferences, podcasts, one-on-one mentoring, listservs, and an extensive website, TAA works to help both new and seasoned authors master their craft. In their second or later year of membership, members may apply for a yearly grant of up to $750 to cover the costs of preparation of a manuscript, including editing, art work, photographic and graphic services, data analysis, publisher charges, and the cost of reprints. TAA also provides initial reviews of publishing contracts. My favorite perk is the annual conference where highly successful authors enjoy helping beginners.

I'm glad you discovered this book. It's a rare opportunity, a pathway you can use to visit the private worlds of writers. *It Works for Me: Becoming a Publishing Scholar/Researcher* and TAA are two tools that you will want to keep at your fingertips. They will enrich your scholarship. Good writing!

Kenneth T. (Ken) Henson
The Citadel

Introduction

Back in 1970 revolutionary Abbie Hoffman believed that his guide for surviving America was so important to disseminate that he called his manifesto *Steal This Book*. Likewise, we believe this book is so important to share with today's audience that we almost called it *Take My Book, Please* [rim shot].

On the other hand, does the scholarly world need another book on the importance of scholarship? Further, if the book standard for tenure is slowly disappearing because so many academic presses are closing, why would we bother to write one? And recent studies show that new faculty members consider university employment a 9:00-5:00 job, so doesn't that leave out time for job-related reading? Finally, with the instant gratification of the internet, aren't books dead in our culture or at least well on their way to extinction?

Why, then, in the name of all that's sane, did we put this collection together?

a. Our publisher wanted a follow-up to our *It Works for Me as a Scholar-Teacher* as he believed we had a lot more to say on the subject.
b. With over 800 publications, we thought we had something insightful to say.
c. Most books on the importance of scholarship are either textbook in nature or extremely theoretical, while this book is neither.
d. With our successful *It Works for Me* series we've found a niche in the marketplace.
e. Being a large collaboration, this book provides many voices who all believe in reiterating the importance of scholarship.
f. With a series of short, practical tips on scholarship, this book is very easy to read and, hence, might be read.

Actually, all of the above are true. But before this Introduction sounds like a 500-word theme or a turn on Browning's "How Do I Love Thee," let's get to something more important: why should you read this book? Let us count the reasons.

A few weeks ago we visited with our university's provost to discuss, among other things, the theme of new faculty orientation (which we run in our capacity as co-directors of the Teaching & Learning Center). Since our last book in the *It Works for Me* series focused on the scholar-teacher, we proposed the academic quest toward becoming a scholar-teacher as the orientation's fundamental and powerful concept. She liked the idea, but given our university's historic focus on teaching (i.e., job one), she suggested we build a week around the teacher-scholar. Her idea was fine with us because our university is not an R-1 institution, but, more importantly, because no matter how the terms "teacher" and "scholar" are hyphenated, they belong together.

Excellent teachers must be excellent scholars, and excellent scholars should carry that expertise into the classroom.

Another good reason not just to read but to use this book is the tenure, promotion, and evaluation policies embedded in higher education. With the supply of instructors greater than the demand in so many fields and with many institutions employing more adjuncts than tenure-track faculty, tenure and promotion standards have become more rigid, and most institutions demand more publications than in the past. While this metamorphosis has been decried as "mission creep," the raised bar for scholarship and research is the new reality.

And how about clarity of thought? When we strove in the trenches as English 101 instructors, we offered as a partial justification for the 10,000 words that we demanded each frosh produce the notion of clear thinking. As English writer E. M. Forster once wrote, "How do I know what I think until I see what I say?" Writing is discovery, a valuable skill that helps us clarify our thoughts. Do you really understand why you're against the NBA's 24-second clock or for reforming the American health care system until you have to translate your sometimes jumbled thoughts into organized prose on paper? Researching and writing for publication helped us articulate why Margot Macomber shot her husband and join in the scholarly conversation with our peers as well as aiding us as we strove to create and develop professional learning communities as a method of faculty development here at Eastern Kentucky University. Likewise, the strategies offered in this book will enhance your ability to clarify your thoughts and use them more efficiently and effectively.

Continually adding to your knowledge base provides another reason for developing your scholarship. After all, as a college instructor, you are in the business of knowledge-making, whether fostering it in others or producing it yourself. Your knowledge ceiling is something you never obtain, for in the words of Tennyson's Ulysses, whom you'll remember we used as a model in our previous book, your goal must ever be "to follow knowledge like a sinking star." Those of you well into your scholarly odyssey recognize that the learning is in the journey, that the final prize is never attained, but that a reason to continue was best expressed by the poet Theodore Roethke with "I learn by going where I have to go." Ulysses had no foreknowledge he would encounter a cyclops or a siren, but those close encounters prepared him for the next leg of his journey. Just so, each step on your journey, while sometimes difficult, prepares you for future challenges. And, as Ulysses had seers and other helpers along his route, the scholars' tips included in this collection can make your travel smoother and more productive.

Since you are in the knowledge biz, your life is not just your own. In every classroom you become a model for young knowledge-seekers. In fact, if you are not performing your own research, you will come across as hypocritical to the very students you are trying to teach. Conversely, if you engage in constant scholarship, you not only have current and personal examples to provide to your students, but you empathize with their scholarly quests. After all, what you wish to develop for yourself is the same as for your students. We call that goal a **scholarly frame of mind**, and it is a skill you must first master before inculcating it in your students. What is a scholarly frame of mind? Stay tuned.

Closely related to this goal is the "publish or perish" metric of higher education. And while most faculty interpret the standard as "if I don't publish, I will be let go from my position," that phrase is open to another interpretation. If you don't publish, what will perish is a scholarly frame of mind, if you ever achieved it in the first place. Certainly, not all scholarship, even scholarship that is worthwhile, will get published, but if you don't try to write it and use it as your entry card into the community of scholars, you will soon discover how terrible an unused mind can be as you forfeit the joy that comes from sharing your findings with colleagues and students, not to mention the satisfaction of personal growth.

Scholarship also reflects another key skill you need to develop and model—**critical thinking**, a skill the business world tells us they want to see in our graduates. We once published an article on why Whitey the Barber in Ring Lardner's "Haircut" was the chief mastermind in the killing of Jim Kendall, and then just to exercise our critical thinking skills, especially our analysis of assumptions, turned around and published an article on Whitey's being the ultimate naïf. We transferred that skill to our students when we had them write back-to-back argument papers; the catch was that whatever side of an issue they argued in paper one, they had to take the other side in paper two. And this critical thinking aspect of research and scholarship not only helped us as lit teachers; it proved crucial as we collaborated with colleagues from across our campus to develop the University's Quality Enhancement Plan (QEP) mandated by SACS, our regional accrediting agency.

We could even argue that it's your duty to become a practicing scholar. When you signed on for the complete academic ride, you tacitly contracted to provide your best as a scholar and model.

Or maybe we should point out that the scholarly club has a small membership. If less than one-half of one percent of Americans has PhDs, twenty years ago Robert Boice pegged the number of practicing scholars at 15% of that. And what part of that subset is self-motivated toward excellence? Want an even smaller subset? Researchers have found that to develop any skill to its fullest, be you a Boston Red Sock or a British Beatle, you need 10,000 hours of what is known as deliberate practice. Before their first hit, the Beatles logged that much time in Hamburg night spots and Liverpool dives.

Logically, to be an excellent scholar, you would need 10,000 hours of scholarly endeavors. Now writing a dissertation helps build up those scholarly hours, but most professors still have a long way to go to reach the 10K standard. Indeed, the fellowship of practicing scholars is small, but the rewards are great.

Legends say that when prize-winning author Sinclair Lewis stood before fawning would-be writers at Yale, he simply stared at the young Elis for a long time, then questioned, "Why aren't you all home writing?" We could ask you the same question, but we'd prefer you read on before beginning your journey or, if you are already well into your career, charting a change in direction. After all, Ulysses' journey home took him ten years and cost him lots of scars—we think this book will get you to your goal of becoming a constantly publishing scholar quicker and without further bruises.

Finally, we need to be up front with our loyal readers. Some of our ideas in this book have appeared in the previous books in the *It Works for Me* series. Think of these books as complements to each other, companion pieces that occasionally overlap because some of our beliefs haven't changed in the series' twelve years. Just as an effective teacher reiterates fundamental and powerful concepts, so we continue to stress certain principles, and, yes, some we pull out intact while others we modify.

More specifically, in this book we have tried to make coherent what began five books ago as a shotgun approach to various areas of the scholar-teacher's life. For the first time we offer a step-by-step guide for your journey; think of this book as an academic GPS navigator with its voice constantly suggesting you turn here ... take this route ... avoid this jam ... be cautious here, and you will reach your destination.

Bon voyage!

Developing A Scholarly Frame of Mind

In our last book, *It Works for Me as a Scholar-Teacher*, we spent some time defining a scholarly frame of mind. We mentioned fine minds like Darwin, Taine, Freud and Jung, even positing the statement, "Nobody remembers a great thinker like J. J. Newberry." The line was a clue of sorts (remember we're also mystery writers), a set-up that we put in the book hoping that someone would call us on it. Google or Bing J. J. Newberry and you'll find a chain-store magnate of the early 20th century, but you won't find a "great thinker," at least not one in the company of Darwin, Taine, *et al*. Thanks to those scholars who asked us about the line.

And that brings us to the pivotal question for this book: exactly what traits belong to this rare individual known as a scholar?

Scholars are curious folk. They question everything, and like Faust they have a desire to know everything, even if on the smaller scale of a discipline.

Scholars are life-long learners, like Chekhov's perpetual student Trofimov in *The Cherry Orchard*. They possess the intellectual humility to realize how little they know.

Scholars emulate Chaucer's clerk—"and gladly wolde he lerne and gladly teche." Teachers cannot teach until they can learn, and even when they teach, they are learning.

Scholars pursue with the zeal of a lover or The Great Detective from 221-B Baker Street.

Scholars read everything with a pen or least they make marginal notations, most often in the form of questions. And they come back to those marginal musings trying to make sense of them individually and collectively.

Scholars synthesize, noting that an image in a Flannery O'Connor story looks a lot like one used by the British poet Yeats and wondering why.

Scholars scramble up and down Bloom's taxonomy like an archeologist on a pyramid, assessing, analyzing, applying, seeking.

Scholars tend to read more than one thing at a time.

Scholars are fascinated by both breadth and depth.

Scholars, therefore, become an expert in some area with the vigor and rigor of an animal claiming territory.

Scholars are never satisfied. For them, there's a sequel and a pre-quel for every story.

Scholars are forensic scientists, seeking every bit of evidence they can find, verifying it, double-checking it, testing it.

Scholars don't have to be told to go forth and multiply, parse, investigate, or discover. They're already going-forth when someone comes to tell them to.

Scholars collect knowledge—books picked up at yard sales, old newspapers and magazines, other people's junk. They sense something lies within the artifact, and they hope at some time they will have the time to come back and solve riddles of lesser sphinxes.

Scholars produce, whether it's a law, a discovery, a new piece of knowledge, an invention, an innovative process, a sonata. A simplicity is seen in their discoveries that makes people say, "Why didn't I think of that?"

Scholars ponder a problem on a subconscious level even when they appear to be cooking dinner, watching a ballgame, teaching a class, or sleeping. Scholars have been known to pin notes to their clothing, put a writing pad beside their bed, or even pull over on an interstate to jot down something that seems important at the time.

Scholars are misunderstood. They show up late because they have been working on something. They zone out in the middle of conversations. They make comments completely irrelevant to conversations. They get criticized for having no hobbies when, in truth, scholarship is their vocation and everything else is an avocation.

Most importantly, scholars are passionate, embracing their work like devoted lovers, for it is this passion that carries them through frustrating, even desperate times.

You probably don't have to be told these characteristics of a scholarly frame of mind. In fact, you look at this essay like a mirror and wonder how someone knows you so well. The community of scholars has always been a small one, but its influence extends disproportionately beyond its size. Still, we would like to see that community expand. We would like to see more individuals develop that scholarly frame of mind and use it to become sustaining, practicing scholars. Since our contributors come from varied disciplines, we have tried to keep their unique styles through a minimum of line editing and have left their individual reference formats intact.

This book contains some advice from the community of scholars who are inviting you to join them.

R.S.V.P.

Hal Blythe
Charlie Sweet
Eastern Kentucky University

Creating Your Scholarly Plan

"A good education is, above all, a habit of mind."

In the 18th century legendary life coach Ben Franklin emphasized the importance of developing a plan for any pursuit, pronouncing, "By failing to prepare, you are preparing to fail." He even established an ethical rubric that he checked off daily to ensure he accomplished his prime goal of leading a virtuous life. In the 20th century legendary basketball coach John Wooden echoed Big Ben's clarion call with "Failure to prepare is preparing to fail." Even our military mnemonicized this guideline through alliteration with the pithy phrase "Prior preparation prevents poor performance." Importantly, no matter how the insight is phrased, the concept of planning is the foundation for a scholarly life.

What we propose is a deliberate, systematized, and coherent scholarly plan. More precisely, the plan proposes guidelines in three areas we have discussed in previous volumes—pre-writing, writing, and post-writing. In the final stage we'll elaborate on ways of sustaining the plan beyond the shelf-life of a New Year's resolution, especially the importance of discipline.

Pre-Writing

Make the deliberate choice to be a scholar, a process that goes beyond graduate course work, researching a dissertation, and getting ready for class. It is a 24/7, active way of life that involves the continuous seeking of knowledge in a methodical way so that you can absorb it, analyze it, build on it, and disseminate it. A true scholar is like your vampire electronic devices (e.g., your TV) ... always on.

How did we publish 800 items in 35 years? Did we say we wanted to average 23 items per year for the next four decades? Did we abandon our families and the classroom and move to a Tibetan monastery to research the wisdom of the ages? Did we strike a bargain with the Devil? No, we began with an open-ness to ideas, an awareness of the world around us, the desire to be overly prepared in the classroom. Truthfully, we never thought of our scholarly pursuits in terms of promotion and tenure. And in the beginning, no, we didn't make a conscious decision to be scholars—we just did it, saw how much we enjoyed it, and only after some early success did we figure out that to continue, to get better, and to thrive, we needed a deliberate plan. We'd like to shortcut our discovery for you.

Like our colleagues, in those early days we could always come up with a thousand reasons not to research and write, but by overcoming our weaknesses from "I don't feel like writing today" to "This isn't working," and making some necessary compromises along the way (yes, the classroom, the family, the church, and even the Little League were also vital parts of our lives), we achieved a scholarly life.

Truthfully, the better we defined and refined components of our plan—and stuck to it—the more scholarly and the more productive we became.

The key to any plan is a goal. As creative writing teachers, we used to emphasize that the essence of fiction was character, and that to write an effective story you had to give your character a goal. In fact, we always forced novice writers to create a fictional biography for their primary characters much like an employment application—except that the fictional bio had to include at the bottom the character's main goal in life. The story was, then, the character's attempt to achieve that goal, be it monetary, romantic, physical, or otherwise.

Start your plan by setting a modest goal; in fact, give yourself an easy victory. On Charlie's first (and what turned out to an only) higher education job, his chair "proposed" a modest goal for him. He asked Charlie during his first year to concentrate on being the best teacher he could (as we said earlier, at our university, teaching has always been job one), but from the second year on he wanted Charlie to turn out simply one publication/year. As Charlie was both a creative writer and a lit/comp teacher, that goal seemed easy to attain.

How did goal-setting work when we first decided to collaborate? In the mid-seventies we were each writing alone and had published a few poems and a few more critical articles without much knowing what we were doing—certainly without a well-conceived plan. For some reason we had avoided that graduate school advice of milking your dissertations to achieve tenure. At one departmental meeting our chair informed us that the university had invested a few million dollars in instructional TV (ITV) equipment and personnel; the only thing missing were scripts to produce. Now we had played doubles tennis together for a couple of years and were card-carrying videophiles. Sitting in the rathskeller one night after a match, we started talking about the university's need and the fact that no one had volunteered. Since we knew the university's acceptance bar was low, we figured we had little to lose by writing scripts on how to answer essay tests, get the most out of the library, and recognize the logical fallacies all around us. We ended up creating a series for English 101 called *Keys to Communication*, for which we wrote 13 scripts. To reflect on our work, we even penned three scholarly articles on ITV; getting the pieces published was an easy victory because at the time so little had been published on the subject (having so few ITV articles out there also made the research easy).

Where do you start? We've had colleagues who began with book reviews for the local paper. A friend of ours began by volunteering to proofread a senior professor's article and write up a "Works Cited" page for it. Collaborating, as we have pointed out in earlier books and will point out later in this one, is a popular launching pad. In fact, did you know the number of authors on a scientific paper has doubled in the last twenty years? In the sciences researchers often plan on working themselves up the step-ladder to primary investigator from as far as twelve rungs below.

Gradually increase your goals. We didn't set out to write the 13+3 package on ITV, but once we finished the creative part, the critical just seemed a natural extension. One thing that always kept us fresh was writing fiction **and** critical works; whenever burn-out threatened us in one field, we could switch to the other.

Focus on the two-fer and three-fer. You always have more research and ideas than you get on paper, so use—don't throw out—your left-overs. When we wrote the first script for the *Keys to Communication* series, we found it fun and easy. Also, with a 4-4 load we were teaching two sections of Freshman English, so ideas for scripts were easy to generate. Hanging around the studio to fine-tune our scripts as they were being shot introduced us to the literature of the field, and between takes we found ourselves glancing through such publications as *Audio-Visual Instructor*. We wrote a piece in that magazine's format, and then turned to our own field and revamped the piece for *College English*.

Keep on constant alert for starter ideas. When a young writer asked the master for advice, Henry James replied, "Try to be one of those people on whom nothing is lost." While the majority of our critical articles came out of some classroom experience, our fiction grew out of a combination of personal experiences (our own and those of friends) and a clip file.

Sometimes while preparing a course lesson, we noticed something we could write about. Charlie was teaching *The Scarlet Letter* for about the twentieth time when he felt something wrong with the novel's timeline. He mentioned it to Hal, they did some research, and a note was born on something scholars had missed for 150 years. One thing that helped us was spending time everyday discussing things of which we had suddenly become aware.

Other times it was the actual class, and it didn't matter whether the class was undergraduate or graduate. Suddenly you catch a glimmer of an idea, like the time while teaching an Intro to World Lit course section on Browning when Hal sensed a similarity in the images used by the Duke in "My Last Duchess." He couldn't synthesize what he "glimpsed," but he jotted down a marginal note that later became a publication in *Studies in Browning*. Sometimes a student asks a question you can't answer. Looking for a possibility after class can become the basis for a piece.

Fiction was different, for just about anything we experienced, read about, saw in the paper or on television offered the germ of a story. Sometimes another piece of fiction demanded a fictional response. We once wrote a detective story wherein we sent Poe's detective Dupin to a haunted house because it was our way of figuring out what really caused "The Fall of the House of Usher." One mystery story was our grafting the pursuit plot of Connell's "The Most Dangerous Game" to a Mike Shayne detective story we had been hired to ghost. Another time we diabolically killed off a villain who just happened to have the last name of our departmental chairman.

Because of the constant bombardment of ideas and images, we eventually evolved a clip file method. Every time we had an idea for a critical article or for a piece of fiction, we jotted down a note or clipped out the article and dropped it in a file folder; for us, the "thrilla" in manila was finding a viable piece of paper to expand into something publishable. The file folder was also great for lean times more when we needed not an idea, but a challenge; once, for instance, we wrote a 20,000-word Mike Shayne novella by weaving a plot from three random pieces of paper pulled out of our fiction ideas file. Right now there's a slip of paper in the file that has been there over twenty years because we have never gotten to it or figured it out (why in Cheever's "The Swimmer" does the narrator make the point that the air smells like cordite after the summer storm Ned Merrill spends in that gazebo?).

Writing

Write and research every day. The fundamental and powerful concept underlying every creative writing class we ever taught is a writer is one who writes. Most scholars and fiction writers confuse writing with idea generation. For years we had a colleague who wanted P&T credit because he sat around and thought deeply for over 20 hours/week. Scholars and writers are people who create product. Remember the traditional monetary offer for your thoughts.

Set a daily objective in terms of time spent/page count, especially when you are getting started. Robert B. Parker—the recently deceased creator of detectives Spenser, Jesse Stone, and Sunny Randall—was very prolific because his goal was to write five pages in the morning and five pages in the afternoon ... every day. When we were ghost-writing the Mike Shayne series as well as teaching our 4/4 load and producing over five critical works per year, we had to produce a 20,000-word novella every month. An average month yields about 20 working days, so we had to set a goal of 1,000 words every day.

Find a spot to write. When we began writing, we shared an office, so that seemed a natural place to write. Unfortunately, the phone would ring, students would drop in, and colleagues would stop by. Eventually we moved to the local McDonald's, where for over twenty years we had our own booth. For the most part people would leave us alone ... unless we were discussing how to commit a fictional murder too loudly. Virginia

Woolf once gave a lecture where she stressed the need for each female writer to have "a room of her own." Technology has made that room virtually anywhere. With a laptop/net book, you can write at a kid's soccer game, the back of the bar, or on the lawn in front of the psych building. Our experience, however, suggests that establishing a single place acts as a stimulus-response way to get your juices flowing.

Carve out some time to write every day. Once we became serious about our writing, we worked out class times with our department chair in order to give us large blocks of time to write. Some semesters we would teach the first two class blocks, and other times we were "goal-posted" by having an 8:00 and a 1:00. In between we drove down to McDonald's. We've had colleagues and students who would either get up very early a la English writer Anthony Trollope or stay up late (a la every grad student in the history of the world). Again, regularity is a virtue in terms of coaxing the writing act ("Hey, it's 5:30 a.m. I've got two hours before breakfast ... time to get the juices flowing").

Post-Writing

Learn how to do market research. Novice scholars often choose a topic that interests them, research it, write the article, and submit it. True, some of these submissions may be published, but the odds are against them. Would McDonald's suddenly build a new store because a piece of land looks good? Would Gillette put out a new razor, the OctoBlade, just because the brand has a nice ring to it? No, in both cases they would study the market. McDonald's would want to know the local demographics, the traffic flow, the propinquity of competitors, etc., while Gillette would probably find a test market for its new product.

In writing you might want to follow the example of Edgar Allan Poe. In order to break into the Gothic tale market of the nineteenth century, he actually studied a popular English publication in this field. His results are found in the essay "How To Write a Blackwood Article," which was not only the first literary market analysis, but our model. When we were trying to get our first story published in *Ellery Queen's Mystery Magazine*, we submitted 25 unsuccessful manuscripts. Realizing we might be doing something wrong ... duh ... we analyzed one full year of stories, actually making a chart about the types of characters and plots preferred, the average story's length, the favored point of view, etc. With our chart in hand we crafted a tale that fell well within **EQMM** tendencies, and the story was published. In the scholarly world we broke into *Studies in Short Fiction* the same way and recently *Academe*.

If you want to write for a journal, read that journal and, more importantly, study it. And instead of considering this idea a post-writing approach, you might think of doing it before you write that first article. If nothing else, at least read a publisher's or a journal's Submission Guidelines (most have a website).

Submit. Some writers suffer from the curse of perfection, and until they feel the article or even a book approaches the ideal state, they keep it encaged in their computer. Other writers can't deal with failure, so no article out, no rejection possible. We used to tell our students that we didn't know of a single story published where the manuscript lay coffined in a desk drawer. Writers used to argue they couldn't afford the necessary stamps, but in an electronic age submission is free.

Rejection and revision are handmaidens of the muse. Now we're going to tell you the truth. First-time submissions, even targeted ones, are most often rejected. Why? In the wonderful world of fiction, "This does not meet our needs" usually means just that: rather than commenting exclusively on the story's quality, the editor might be saying your piece is not of proper length or appropriate subject matter (ah, the importance of market research). In the scholarly world of refereed publications, rejection usually comes with a checklist and often a peer reviewer's comments about your work. Study the rejection until you can devise the necessary steps to raise your work up to the required standards for publication. What was missing in your manuscript? A central argument? Textual evidence? Research that overlooked Scholar X?

Revise along the lines of what you have been told. Some beginners' submissions miss the mark by a lot, and the argument has to be recast. Some hypotheses don't pan out. Most need additional research because they missed something key or something current. And make friends with an English professor to help you through the grammatical maze.

Learn the Staircase Approach. All of us want to see our work in top-tier journals and magazines. As budding mystery writers, we sought the Holy Grail of *Ellery Queen's Mystery Magazine*, and as would-be famous literary critics, we wanted to see our scholarship between the covers of *PMLA*. But we didn't start there. Our first published mysteries were in fanzines, a now-discontinued Canadian publication, and finally *Mike Shayne Mystery Magazine*. Our early attempts at lit crit were reworkings of bad term papers that had been written the night before they were due. We even published a couple of things (one on sportscasters' misuse of the language) in a local paper, but they saw print and we were often even paid.

For you, publication might begin with a campus presentation. We did a workshop for our department on publishing that we turned into an article. Several other publications grew out of presentations at our Teaching & Learning Center. And we have published materials that grew out of committee work and learning communities.

Or your article might start as a conference presentation. Most disciplines have an annual statewide conference. Be a presenter, and rather than praise, seek out honest criticism of what you could do to enhance your argument. Revise and consider trying a regional conference. Again, revise and take your show on the road to the national meeting. National meetings are also a great place to meet notable scholars in your field as well as editors. Seek them out. Some will shoo you away like an obnoxious gnat, but all you need is the help of one. At a conference in Nashville we ran into the editor of a popular magazine who sat down with us and over lunch told us exactly what he was looking for in fiction. At the John D. MacDonald Conference in Florida we met JDM himself, and he helped open some doors in the field. At the Lilly Conference on Teaching and Learning we have met several editors who have helped us transition into the field of educational research.

Penultimately, if you are just starting, seek out senior faculty who publish as mentors. Offer to help them with a piece. See if they will help you with an idea you have or look over a draft. We have also written authors of stories and articles that we have liked. Our correspondence with them over the years has made us better. Early in our mystery-writing career we made friends with an assistant editor who was constantly rejecting our stories. By the time he became the editor of the magazine, he had grown us as writers and was happy to publish us.

Finally, follow the path we give to our students. In our middle- to upper-division classes, instead of term papers, we have our students create publishable notes. Since a note is around 1500 words in our discipline, students learn to write articles in miniature, and they learn to be concise. In an American Lit course we show the students some examples of relevant journals, and we break down the notes into their components. And, every semester we model the note; if the student is writing a note, so are we. We use our note-writing as an example by taking students from the first glimpse of an idea, to the research, to the writing, and to the revision. Students then submit one copy to us and one to their journal of choice. Over the years several of our students started their publishing careers with successful submission of their notes.

Keep an inventory. With the first article you write, you will live and breathe with its progress, but once you have more than one, you will start to lose track. When we became publishing maniacs back in the 80s, we had times when we had over thirty articles/stories out there (unpublished manuscripts seem to multiply like rabbits and tribbles when you are beginning), and we could no longer remember what was where or even what stage the piece was in. Now with computers you can keep electronic files of all drafts. Here's a hint: finish all your Word files with a dot followed by that date so that you can always tell which document is the most current version of the work. Also, maintain a large file called **INVENTORY** in which you name the WORK, the DATE you submitted it, and the work's DISPOSITION. Perhaps because we're old school, we keep a paper folder with the final draft, the correspondence, and the research. The latter is important because sooner or later we always come back to certain stories to write still another article (we have published over ten articles on John Cheever's "The Swimmer" and another ten on Bobbie Ann Mason's "Shiloh"), and we need our collected research as a launching pad.

Summary

Having a good plan is never enough. You must be disciplined to follow it. No, you probably don't need a Ben Franklin-type rubric and checklist. On the other hand, when we started diet and exercise programs, that's exactly what we had to do. When we help each other on a house project such as constructing a deck or pool house, we keep a step-by-step do-list, especially since we're not experts in diet, exercise, or construction. Research shows that people who are internally motivated are more likely to be self-disciplined, so perhaps the entire key to a scholarly plan comes down to one question: do I truly wish to lead a scholarly life?

If the answer is yes, welcome to the conversation.

Overviews

With something as career-significant as your scholarly plan, you would probably feel more certain if you received advice from more than one source—albeit the Co-Oracles of Richmond. To satisfy your desire for corroboration (a necessary disposition for a scholar-researcher), we've gathered sage comments from colleagues from hither and yon concerning approaches to becoming a publishing scholar. You'll note that their comments often overlap—and that's a positive thing since such repetition affirms the strategy's validity and helps you learn it. Our colleagues come from a variety of disciplines and positions—some are administrators and some reside outside the purely academic zone—but all have successfully published, many outside their discipline.

Devour what they bring to the table, and don't be afraid to take seconds.

Getting Published: Inquiring Minds Want to Know

Have you ever heard that it is "publish or perish" for those seeking to obtain tenure or promotion in the ivory towers? Has the question come to mind, how do I get published? The truth is, inquiring minds of young professors entering the academy want to know? The constant fear or anxiety of "to publish or perish" for many new faculty members as they navigate in the academy is a reality. Entering a place of the "unknown," with "no guidance," "no mentoring," and "no support," many become frustrated and some even leave without accomplishing this milestone.

In a climate in which faculty accountability is ever more dependent on research and scholarship, especially as rewarded by promotion and tenure, improvement in the quality of teaching is an increasing concern (Pearson & Thomas, 2009). It is important to note, research informs our teaching practices and that institutions should provide the necessary support for such an endeavor. As Jacobs (1998) asserts, "institutional culture can be a vehicle for improving satisfaction and productivity." This tip will provide a roadmap for a successful publishing experience and a compass that one may utilize when seeking support or mentoring through this process.

Process: Where to Begin?

Becoming a proficient, efficient, and effective writer requires discipline. It requires management of both yourself and your time. It requires focus on the topic or discipline studied. It is necessary to revisit your thesis/dissertation in order to extract or to expand relevant research areas. Liken the publishing experience to a relationship. After a disagreement, you may have a desire to remove yourself from the writing piece all together (*your committee*), never returning to write on the topic again. Similarly, you may liken the experience to childbearing. You birth the child and endure the pain and agony of the event. Next, you have the desire to make all the right decisions and choices necessary for the child's success, only to discover your child requires more work. Later, after reflecting on the hard work, time, resources, and passion, you return to find ways to enhance, advance, and nurture it to the next place called "success." So where to begin? Begin by exploring journals you visited while developing your thesis/dissertation. Identify areas that peak your interest and capture the theme of the journal. Follow the guidelines provided by the journal's editorial staff and you will be well on your way to publishing.

Drive: How To Gain Momentum?

Network with other scholars to converse and mutually exchange ideas and share experiences. Faculty development is an effective way to foster the spirit of collegiality and community. Zahorski (2002) purports, "The synergistic approach helps create an environment of hope and opportunity, the kind of environment in which scholarship has the best chance of thriving. Like the dynamic space Elwin Ransom discovers while journeying to Malacandra, it can be a living nurturing environment, that lifts the spirits, engenders hope, encourages and supports risk-taking and innovation, and inculcates a spirit of cooperation and collaboration" (p.37).

Assess your research for any emerging themes to explore from multiple perspectives. Collect additional supportive evidence and identify a mentor who may share your same research interest. Your colleagues may be your best resource for where to submit your research. Keeping in mind faculty mentors have various talents, it is important, as Boyer (1990) asserts, to support the various kinds of scholarship in order to enhance the academic learning community. Mentoring is necessary! Members of the professoriate experience periods of stability and periods of change. But for faculty, such ebbs and flows are profoundly influenced and complicated by imposed barriers and politics in higher education. Therefore, having a mentor to provide a listening ear and psychosocial support as a form of relational learning can be extremely valuable (Pearson, 2007).

Passion: How To Deal With Revise & Resubmit?

Thanks for that INVALUABLE info about how revise/resubmit requests are not rejections. I recently had a 15 page manuscript ACCEPTED to *The History Teacher*. The revise/resubmit emails seemed so "cold" that I would have interpreted it as rejection had I not known this "reading between the lines" secret. THANK YOU!!! (A new faculty).

Do not view a revise and resubmit as a rejection. Take a step back from the document for a few days. Review your writing style, address any feedback, and identify areas for improvement in your writing. If necessary, send your manuscript to other colleagues to serve as editors. Consider hiring an editor who has strong technical writing skills. Keep your passion alive and remember, no pain, no gain! You will gain from a journal that will serve as a vehicle for disseminating new knowledge. You will gain as a contributing member to your discipline, and you will gain from the public recognition and the respect of your peers in academia. At this point, you are ready to resubmit.

Perseverance: How To Deal With Rejection?

Learn to accept rejection and allow yourself to heal from the disappointing news that your manuscript was not accepted. Be prepared to resubmit to a less prestigious journal and have the ability to reply to criticism rationally. Brainstorm about ideas to add to the literature. Reevaluate the research, the methodology section, and look for gaps. Write for clarity and a broad audience. Examine the depth and breadth of the research. Make connections between current research, theory and practice, lived experiences, and teaching pedagogy. Remember you are not the victim, but the victor of publishing your research and scholarly work.

Conclusion

In conclusion, successful writers must understand that writing is a process. In order to get published, you must develop the drive, fuel your passion, and stay your course to persevere. It is important to realize that writing is a way to self-educate and increase your personal knowledge base, as well as providing more knowledge to your audience. Inquiring minds may want to know how to get published, but the truth of the matter is, you possess all the necessary skills to accomplish and answer your own question.

References

Boyers, E.(1990). *Scholarship reconsidered: New priorities for the professoriate*. San Francisco: Jossey-Bass.

Jacobs, F. (1998). Using part-time faculty more effectively. In D.M. Leslie (Ed.), The growing use of part-time faculty: Understanding causes and effects. *New Directions for Higher Education* (Vol. 104, pp. 9-18). San Francisco: Jossey-Bass.

Pearson, M., and Thomas, K. (2009) Promoting the wholesome professor: Building, sustaining and assessing faculty. In S. E. Van Kollenburg, (Ed.) *A Collection of Papers on Self- Study and Institutional Advancement 2009: Accountability and Organizational Leadership* 1(1), 109-111. Chicago, IL: Higher Learning Commission.

Pearson, M. (2007). Mentoring, modeling, & growing your own. *Higher Learning Commission: A Collection of Papers on Self-Study and Institutional Improvement,* 1(4), 130-134.

Zahorski, K. (2002). Nurturing scholarship through holistic faculty development: A synergistic approach. In K. Zahorski (Ed.), Scholarship in the Postmodern Era: *New Venues, New Values, New Visions. New Directions for Teaching and Learning,* No. 90 (pp. 29–37). San Francisco: Jossey-Bass.

Mildred Pearson
Beverly Cruse
Eastern Illinois University

The Not-So-Obvious Strategies to Become A Publishing Research Scholar

The following strategies were developed over time and have been beneficial in developing as a publishing research scholar. An essential component to this development is embracing the act and procedure of publishing. If one can accomplish this process, then with each research project the entire process becomes easier from question development to dissemination. Seeking out research opportunities, making connections, knowing your audience, and openness to writer's block are just a few techniques that when utilized can increase your ability and skills as a publishing research scholar.

Perhaps the simplest strategy is taking advantage of opportunities at your disposal. For example, most if not all institutions and organizations have newsletters or other publication materials seeking manuscripts. These types of publications will help develop writing to a specific audience, writing in a concise fashion, working with editors, and following submission guidelines. In most cases, these publications have a faster turn-around rate to receive feedback and improve skill. Moreover, many institutions have faculty development programs that provide guidance to developing researchers. Participating in these programs can introduce novice researchers to more experienced faculty and begin mentoring or other research partnerships.

Making connections is another helpful technique. Schedule a meeting with your institution's human subjects review board to fully understand the process for submitting research proposals. Missing a human subjects review board submission deadline can possibly delay your research months. Knowing the kind of review (for example, exempt, expedited, or full review), submission dates, and needed requirements will keep your research on track and increase its likelihood of a timely publication. In addition to mastering the human subjects review process, seek out journal editors and reviewers on your campus or at conferences to gain insider insights. Certain editors will review manuscripts and provide feedback before you officially submit your work. This extra level of feedback can provide valuable information on your manuscript's appropriateness and help in deciding where you ultimately submit your work. Also becoming a journal reviewer is another excellent means to improve your own skills.

Before you start writing, know your audience. In other words have an idea where you would like to submit your manuscript before you begin writing. Having this knowledge can help throughout the writing process. For example, each publication has its own language and terminology. When writing outside of your discipline, you may have to spend more time defining terms and justifying research methodologies than you would inside your discipline. It is also important to know journal submission guidelines. It can be very irritating editing your work because you did not know there was a word count or you wrote your manuscript in APA style and the journal requires manuscripts in Chicago style. Finally, having an awareness of the journal's manuscript acceptance rate and timeline for publication can provide valuable information in choosing the best outlet for your work. This last point is perhaps most important for individuals who are on the tenure track. If accepted articles have a two year waiting period for publication, perhaps another outlet would better suit your promotion and tenure needs.

Embrace the fact that you will encounter periods of writer's block. Embracing writer's block can help decrease the frustration of not feeling productive when words are not flowing from your finger tips. Even writing only one sentence is better than not writing at all. In other words, be content with any effort directed towards your project. Simply write, write, and write some more; with the ease of word processing it is not necessary to find the perfect words the first time you begin writing. Editing your work is another way to remain productive when you are in the midst of writer's block. It is also helpful to employ multiple edits, with each edit focusing on a different aspect of your work (for example, content, grammar, writing style, manuscript guidelines, etc). Breaking editing down into individual tasks can help ensure a detailed examination of your work and ultimately a better final product. As with the entire research process, the more you write the easier it will be to develop and you will soon discover your own techniques to diminish writer's block.

Seeking out research opportunities, making connections, knowing your audience and openness to writer's block have the potential to transform your emerging ability as a publishing research scholar to expert status. Moreover, actively utilizing this text to discover other strategies and tips will only enhance your research ability. Finally, take stock in the fact you took a step forward in your development by reading this text. Perhaps your willingness to improve your skill is your greatest talent to become a publishing research scholar.

Michael Kiener
Maryville University, St. Louis

Tips for Being Published in Academic Journals

Having papers published in professional journals is one of the best ways for us, as scholars, to become recognized within our fields. Whether you are a graduate student new to the field or a professional with decades of experience, being published in a scholarly journal or textbook builds your reputation and opens you up to new opportunities. The importance of being published also contributes to making it a highly competitive and challenging process. Here are some helpful tips to make an aspiring author's work more likely to be published. These tips are presented chronologically, as a step-by-step guide.

Developing the Concept

Three primary elements are critical to keep in mind when developing the idea for an article: relevance, conformity, and requirements. A sound, *relevant* concept is more likely to appeal to prospective readers than one that simply interests you. Journals are unlikely to consider an idea they perceive as narrow and potentially boring. Instead, think about your article from the point of view of the audience. Make sure that it will relate to topics or issues that they care about. You should also invest time in reading the journals to which you intend to submit your article. Knowing the kind of content typically published and the style of writing preferred can help you to *conform* your article to editors' needs and maximize the chance of it being published. The final element is basic: know the publication's word limit and any other *requirements* they may have for authors. An article that does not adhere to a journal's rules demonstrates inadequate research and suggests that you did not put in the time and effort necessary to create a satisfactory submission.

The Article Itself

The most difficult skill in writing a publishable article that you can be proud of is the actual writing involved. First, you must choose a title that is interesting and reflects the subject of the article. A good title will draw in the reader and entice him or her to actually read your article. Likewise, a good opening is critical.

In drafting the body of your article, write so that any reasonably literate individual will be able to read and understand it. A good rule is to write so that it will be intelligible to an average first-year college student. This standard means being clear and direct, and avoid using jargon. If your article is good, readers will appreciate your intelligence; it is unnecessary to try to impress them by using big words.

You can make your article more interesting to its readers by relating it to their everyday experiences. Making the material relevant is critical, whether through examples, specific cases, or stories. The more technical the material, the more difficult this approach is, but also the more impressive it will be when you do it well. You should also be thinking about who is going to be reading your article in every step of the writing process. Scholarly journals have reviewers who read your article to decide if it is acceptable. While writing, anticipate any difficulties or questions they may have with your article and write to preempt any possible objections and answer any questions with facts or logic.

Articles for journals should always be shaped like an hourglass: broad at the top and bottom, and narrowly focused in the middle. Begin by discussing what has already been studied concerning your topic, follow with your research, and close with the implications of your work. You should also make your article as concise and to-the-point as possible. Longer articles are more difficult to get published. Space in scholarly journals is a hot and limited commodity. Providing the same information in a half page as someone else submits in a whole page makes you more likely to get the space.

One thing that every good writer must be focused on is the primary message you want the reader to take from your article. When finished, a reader should know what the point of the article was and be able to relate what s/he has gained from having read it.

The Review and the Submission

The more people who read your article, and the more feedback you receive, the more likely your article is to be published. Feedback from multiple reviewers helps ensure that your article will be understandable for a wide range of readers. Difficult as it is, try not to take any feedback defensively. Your reviewers want to help by providing the best advice that they can. Receive their comments gratefully, and take everything into consideration when editing your article.

Before submitting your article, be sure to have it proofread by some of your colleagues. Your final product should be perfect and free of any misspellings or grammatical errors. Once you are finished and checked for accuracy, carefully select a short list of the journals to which you wish to submit it. You should pick journals that reflect what your finished article is about, with a readership that will be receptive to your information.

Submitting your article does not mean that your work is over. Many journals have what is known as a re-submission process. This step occurs when they consider your work to be good, but require you to make some revisions before they will publish it. If your article needs to be resubmitted, be sure to explain to the publisher how you addressed each of the required revisions. Providing the rationale for why you made some changes and did not make others demonstrates your commitment to your work, and can substantially improve its chances of being published.

In summary, writing an article can be an exhilarating, exhausting process, but one that is well worth the effort. Writing is such challenging work because it involves higher-order thinking skills, and honestly, those skills are sometimes a little rusty because we don't use them everyday. Know yourself regarding the writing process itself and what style works best for you to combat writer's block and work through difficult passages and transitions. Work with editors, not against them. And finally, and perhaps most importantly, keep persevering even when rejection letters line your office walls. Hard work, perseverance, and continual learning and improving will pay off for you in the form of an "accepted for publication" letter.

References

Labaree, R. (2004) *Tips for getting published in scholarly journals: strategies for academic librarians.* American Library Association. http://www.ala.org/ala/mgrps/divs/acrl/publications/crlnews/2004/mar/gettingpublished.cfm.

O'Neill, B. (1990) *To get published in a professional journal.* Cooperative Extension System, http://www.joe.org/joe/1990fall/tt2.php

Sternberg, R. (2000) *Guide to Publishing in Psychology Journals.* New York: Cambridge University Press.

Robert Mattson
Sara Zachary
Jessica Rickard
Elise Shaffer
Kadie Fritz
Dede Wolfarth
Spalding University

Academic Publishing From An Unknown Regional University

Defining the Problem

Before I came to the university level, I had published some articles, a few in "good" journals. Those articles came from an issue in the school system that triggered inspiration. The inspiration drove the research and the writing, creating a synergy that felt good. Of course, writing was not my job as a school district administrator. When I had an article in print, I was usually marked down in my evaluation because that was "work that university professors should be doing."

Then I became a university professor. My chairperson explained to me that I would be evaluated on my teaching, scholarship and service. Suddenly, publication was actually in my job description.

My previous publications would not count in my yearly reviews, I was surprised to hear. As an administrator, I am trained to believe in systems, and I believed that I needed one.

The First Step to the System

During my first year, I taught nine different courses and wrote one article. The article went to a state journal. The publication was probably a mercy placement by the editor, whom I knew, rather than the result of a carefully crafted, well-researched piece of scholarship. But, I had an article in print for the review and a folder full of ideas.

My system began to develop when Ken Henson (2005) came to the University to do a workshop on writing for publication. I can't remember all that he taught us that day, but I did pick up ideas from him that helped me begin thinking of a system. Ken helped me establish a sense of intentionality—a strategy to both plan and place the scholarship. (The latter is often missing from faculty members' plans as I review their scholarly agenda during promotion and tenure meetings.)

Fleshing Out the System: Gathering Hints from Proficient Writers

As a former English teacher, I knew that many authors keep an "idea folder," someplace where they toss ideas that occur, often at odd times. An idea folder can have scraps of paper, napkins, and notes in margins of the agenda of a boring meeting. The idea folder became an essential part of my system.

About this time, I read an excellent article by a friend, John Barnitz. As good as the article was, there was no new information in the article. I thought journal articles had to be new information. Not so, he told me. Some information is so important that it "needs to be said and re-said."

Further, John Barnitz had article-after-article out in journal-after-journal. I asked him how he did that. He said that he used a "pipeline approach." He tried to have one article in press, one in submission, and one in preparation at all times. That way, if an article missed, there would be another coming down the pipeline.

Then John gave me perhaps the most important gift—a strategy. He said that he worked on one research project in a semester. For example, in January, he would state the problem and conduct the review of literature. In February, he would establish the research design. In March, he would conduct the research. In April, he would write the results. In May, he would polish the article and send it out. His process may have been more elaborate, but these steps became my "take away" because suddenly I could see how to break a large project down into its parts. Each part, in turn, led to the next, making an imposing project easier to tackle. Starting a large project is hard, but starting part of a large project? Not so hard.

Soon after this conversation, I asked another professor about his research agenda. He gave me the best response I have ever gotten. He said, "I've just gotten very curious about curiosity."

That statement was so powerful that I spent a year or two thinking about curiosity. Then I realized that part of the sentence wasn't the important part. The important part was the stem of the sentence—"I've just gotten very curious about ...."

I asked Ken Henson recently how he chose one idea to work out of all that occurred to him.

He shrugged his shoulders and said, "I pick the one that looks the most interesting."

Curiosity drives interest, which drives the research and writing.

System results:
Over the next years, I was able to maintain a scholarly life, getting curious about how school custodians approach their jobs to how principals network. In fact, recently I had a doctoral student contact me to ask for my original research on the latter. She said that as far as she could tell, I was the first researcher to explore networking among women principals. It was not my intention to chart new territory. I just got curious.

Here is to your curiosity!

My System at a Glance:
- Keep an idea folder of items that make you say, "Hum, I wonder...."
- If nothing in the idea folder really triggers your curiosity, then pick what looks most interesting.
- Keep the audience in mind—find the specific journal where this idea might be of interest. (I use the appendices in Henson, 2005.)
- Some things are so important, they need to be said and re-said, so think about a topic that has not been visited in the journals in a while.
- One semester—one project.
- Use the pipeline approach.

References
Henson, K. (2005). *Writing for Publication.* Boston: Pearson.

Darrell Garber
Kutztown University

Maintaining Scholarsip in a Teaching-Focused Institution

Introduction

Across the developmental spectrum of students, teaching is a noble profession. From the brightly decorated walls of preschool classrooms to the formal lecture halls of higher education, passionate teachers make a difference in their students' lives. Some of us are fortunate enough to work in teaching-focused higher education positions where our administrators value and reward high quality education at the post-secondary level. However, the vast majority of the time, internal and external pressures abound for us to maintain respectable scholarly records despite demanding teaching schedules. This is particularly difficult for those of us trained in research-focused universities, with research labs, extramural funding, expensive technology, and highly motivated graduate students. Related, many of us have not had a mentor or infrastructure to develop a line of research in a teaching-focused institution.

Despite the challenges of operating in environments that do not necessarily support or reward individual scholarship efforts, maintaining a successful research agenda is critical to our success in academia. The culture of academia has shifted from an environment where professors work at the same institution for numerous years to one where professors frequently change institutions, especially early in their academic career. Therefore, for our own ability to move across and up university structures, producing quality scholarship is vital for our individual success as well our institutional reputation.

Faculty members might find it necessary to adapt the nature of their scholarship activity to fit their academic institution's specific ecology. Fortunately, this is possible, as many forms of scholarship can be pursued that meet the standards (e.g., peer-review) maintained by most universities for purposes of tenure and promotion evaluation. We can demonstrate a productive line of research without publishing every year in a high impact factor journal. For those of us trained in a research-focused university, we often received the message that any publications outside the "flagship" journals of our respective professions are a waste of time. However, not everyone agrees with this philosophy.

The following is a list, though hardly comprehensive, of scholarly options available to faculty who work under conditions that are not favorable to conventional, empirical research:

Adapting Scholarship to Teaching-Focused Institution

- Examine your research interests/passions and your resources. Determine which ones are more feasible considering lab space, student support, access to relevant populations of interest, technology required, and teaching loads. You will be limited in the

type and quantity of data collection methods available. However, you <u>can</u> still answer research questions about which you are most passionate.
- Meet with your chair or supervisor regularly to discuss departmental priorities in balancing the competing demands of scholarship, teaching, and service. You may have more flexibility than you think.
- Review the publication records of colleagues at your institution and seek out the more successful among them for advice.
- Consider textbook authorship, either as author or editor on a collaborative project.
- Write a book review. Many academic disciplines publish critical reviews of state-of-the-art texts or trade books; indeed, some disciplines publish journals specifically dedicated to such reviews (e.g., *Contemporary Psychology*).
- Write conceptual/theoretical articles.
- Explore conducting reviews of sizable literatures, including formal meta-analyses. Such summaries are increasingly seen as useful scientific stock taking when considerable research on a topic has been conducted. These projects do not require the same costs and technology of traditional data collection. However, they can greatly impact your field. Additionally, undergraduate and graduate students may wish to be involved in these projects.
- Write textbook ancillaries, such as Instructor's Manuals, Student Study Guides, PowerPoint slides, test banks, etc. Many textbook publishers hire free-lance authors to write such ancillaries, which are now packaged along with the texts themselves.
- Find and utilize pre-existing data sets collected by governmental agencies. Governmental agencies share numerous databases that are free or cost nominal fees for researchers to access.
- Present your research at conferences to network with others interested in similar research. Even though your particular study may not be publishable in a highly circulated journal, getting your name "out there" opens doors to collaborate with others with more resources.

Combining Teaching and Scholarship via SoTL

Noted psychologist, B. F. Skinner (1956), once observed that "...college teaching is the only profession for which there is no professional training, and it is commonly argued that this is because our graduate schools train scholars and scientists rather than teachers" (p. 221). This state of affairs has changed little in the half century since his observation, but exciting indicators of change abound on many campuses, especially those with a strong teaching mission. Combining their enthusiasm for teaching with their training as researchers, increasing numbers of faculty are engaged in the Scholarship of Teaching and Learning (SoTL). SoTL can take many forms, depending on the interests of the faculty member, and can include empirical research on the following topics:

- Effective pedagogical strategies – lecture vs. active learning tactics, use of service and/or experiential learning, differing delivery systems (e.g., traditional semester vs. intensive, brief formats)
- Technology in the classroom – although most SoTL research may have a primarily pedagogical focus (role of technology in learning outcomes), additional issues surrounding classroom technology (e.g., cell phone and internet use by students, etc.) are of interest as well
- Assessment of learner outcomes – formative (frequent) vs. summative assessment, rote memorization vs. application, knowledge vs. skills assessment, etc.

SoTL is garnering greater support and recognition within many disciplines, perhaps due to the heightened emphasis on standards of best practice and enhanced accountability accruing to most professionals, including teachers at all levels. Growth in scholarship of teaching and learning may very well be a timely and appealing focus for college faculty whose teaching practices are, justifiably, being placed under the microscope.

Conclusion

An academic position at a teaching-focused institution is truly an honor, but it is not without its challenges and limitations. We hope that the aforementioned strategies are helpful in expanding your view of scholarship and motivating you to pursue your passions beyond the classroom.

References

Skinner, B. (1956). A case history in scientific method. *American Psychologist ,11*, 221-233.

Nate Mitchell
DeDe Wolfarth
David Morgan
Spalding University

Dave's Hints for Publishing

After I have completed the first draft of any paper that I am considering publishing, and before I do any fine-tuning on the final draft, I always try to engage in the following steps that I learned at a seminar delivered at the Southern Sociological Society meetings in the mid-1990's from Patricia Yancey Martin, a fine scholar in her own right. Since I began following her advice in the late 1990s (I'm a slow learner), I have decreased my rejections dramatically. At first glance, these tips might seem like "cheating." I would disagree, however, and would argue that using these hints to win the publishing "game" is much like going on the Internet prior to working on your car and reading advice from master mechanics who are willing to share their "tricks of the trade" with you.

1. Before you start fine-tuning your paper, determine the journal to which you will submit and obtain the guidelines for that journal. Follow them as closely as possible. Remember, editors are people too. If you make their job easier from the outset, they are more likely to be kind to you when they are making their final decision.
2. Find hard or electronic copies of that journal for the last decade and cite any article remotely related to your paper. One of the methods through which journals are ranked for prestige has to do with the number of times articles from that journal are cited. Every editor wants to make his/her journal more prestigious; publishing your article that cites his/her journal many times is an easy way for them to increase the prestige of their journal quickly.
3. Use a journal search engine to search for the names of the journal's editor and review board, and, if they have written articles or books that pertain to your work, cite them in your paper. Every scholar likes to see his/her name appear in print; there is a good chance these individuals may be one or more of your reviewers.
4. Finally, write an explicit cover letter describing your paper. Let the editor know how many pages and how many words your article includes, and explicitly state that you tried to follow the guidelines they suggest on their website (e.g., APA, MLA). Again, this action lets the editor know you have actually read the author's guidelines for submission and cared enough to follow those guidelines.

Hopefully, these hints will help you much like they helped me. Good luck in your scholarship journey.

David May
Eastern Kentucky University

My Story

I have had two books accepted for publication by Jason Aronson of Rowman & Littlefield publishers that will be out soon. It has been a long journey to get published, but the following worked for me:

1. **Timing**: what you publish should be current and add to the field. In my field, for instance, the topic of metaphor was not as popular five years ago when I started trying to publish, but in the last couple of years a number of volumes has come out. Trauma-

focused books and play-therapy techniques have also been popular in the last couple of years.
2. **Competition**: provide a publisher the opportunity for competition with another publishing house. Send your proposal to a publisher that publishes similar topics, but who does not yet have a listing in this area.
3. **Market Research**: piggyback on books the publisher has already accepted for publication in terms of audience, theme, and/or topic. Wander through book stores! Check out Amazon.com to see who has published books similar to the one you are writing.
4. **Twist**: your book needs to add something to other books already in the field. Perhaps it can be used with a different population; perhaps it is a more in-depth application of something already in another book.
5. **Proposal Research**: do your research ahead of time. You need to be persuasive in your proposal and have excellent justification. You need to know other books in that area that have been published recently and tell them why yours is a sellable commodity.
6. **Write**: do the writing up front before you submit your proposal. If you have a well-edited, well-written, nearly finished book that fills a publishing niche, the whole process goes quite smoothly, and there are fewer delays.

Pat Pernicano
Licensed Clinical Psychologist

When Life Intervenes: How to be Academically Productive While Being Biologically Reproductive

Academia's rewards are plentiful, including meaningful, creative work that challenges us to be lifelong learners. But as parents who are also professors, we have found this career path's most useful benefit to be its flexibility. Unfortunately, this flexibility demands a toll: the perpetual anxiety caused by a shadow monster named "Publish or Perish." Academicians' quest for promotion, tenure, and merit raises hinges on our ability to secure grants and publish in peer-reviewed journals. Ironically, however, the time when most newly-minted professors finish their doctoral education and obtain their first position is also the time when our biological clock, or that of our partners, nears its eleventh hour. This situation is not a "women's problem." First of all, more women are earning doctorate degrees than ever before and will eventually surpass the number of men earning doctorates. Second of all, more women in general are entering the workforce, with the number of female employees in the United States, for the first time in history, now greater than the number of male employees (Shriver, 2009). But labeling the need to balance work and family responsibilities as a problem that affects only individuals with two X chromosomes is a misnomer indeed. Today's working men also strive to balance work and family life and report great joy, satisfaction, and value in their role as fathers (Halpern, 2005).

Thus the challenge becomes balancing not just work and family, but juggling these demands at their most intensive times. Taking care of infants and small children requires more time and effort than raising older children (although clearly parenting teenagers requires special patience!). Likewise, publishing at the assistant and associate professor level is more imperative to being granted tenure and moving up the ranks of academia than is publishing as a tenured, full professor. Is this balancing act even possible? And if so, how?

While we do not have "the" answers, we have a few tips that have worked for us. We'll list our advice in convenient bullet-statement style out of recognition that our target readers, the busiest among you, have time to only scan this article:

- Keep your priorities clear. For example, as the deadline for a submission draws near, your work may be more important *at that moment* than your family. But have those moments be few and keep your family first as often as you can.
- Find a mentor whom you respect at your institution and who is willing to let you coauthor for publication. This person can advise you in navigating the political landscape at your university and help you decipher your university's "real" scholarship expectations. Don't be above riding on someone else's coattails; you can extend the favor to someone else later on and pay it forward.
- Find a mentor beyond your institution who is willing to extend his/her help as well; having people outside your cloistered halls is invaluable.
- Consider publishing in the Scholarship of Teaching and Learning area instead of, or in addition to, your content expertise area. The literature in this area is more forgiving compared to some other fields, and action-based research is typically acceptable.
- Consider "brief reports" in higher-tier journals. These journals often accept short and tidy publications that are meaningful but don't quite have the methodological sophistication demanded of a full-length manuscript.
- Be willing to compromise. While peer-reviewed, tier-one journals are the gold standard, publications in "lesser" journals typically count toward your scholarship track record as well, in addition to boosting your confidence. The phrase "Accepted for publication" may not be as sweet as "It's a healthy baby!" but it isn't too far behind. Of course, the relative merit of publications is institutionally driven, with some universities placing weight only on publications with a high impact factor or citation index.

- Make the right sacrifices. Something DOES have to give: we hope it's not your families and loved ones, but perhaps your housekeeping standards, exercise regime, or commitments that aren't particularly important to you. So delegate, even if others don't do things exactly as you would do them. Likewise, say no to some requests for your time, even if it is hard. Boundaries create space, and we need this space to be productive.
- Don't be too hard on yourself. Your children won't suffer permanent developmental damage if they watch an occasional TV program while you work.
- Learn to delegate. Good graduate assistants are worth their weight in academic gold. Yes, it takes time to train these people, but once they learn, they can greatly boost your productivity. Make sure you reward them, however, with co-authorship, regular praise, and gift certificates to practical places that broke graduate students frequent (e.g., fast food restaurants, discount stores, and gas stations).
- Don't make editors into enemies. Despite the messages you may have heard, not all editors are jerks. Ask for help politely and frequently and let your kindness ring through in every email. You will often be amazed what good human beings most people are.
- Always remind yourself of the mantra: It is not a mountain; it is ten small hills. You have written a voluminous dissertation. You can write a ten-page paper. Break it into small chunks, or even microscopic ones, and commit to writing a little bit on a regular basis.
- And finally, don't fuss over perceptions. We are going to have gaps in our vitae. Those gaps are actually babies. And they are worth it.

As we conclude this article, we would like to share a poem that one of us (DW) wrote:

> Razor-like Focus
> Biologic productivity
> Academic productivity
> Inherent multitasking:
> the "razor like focus"
> needed to publish
> isn't always consistent with life.
>
> Who, then, in the razor families
> notices we're low on milk?
> Or arranges emergency babysitting
> or ensures the van has the right car seats,
> the diaper bag is stocked,
> and the kids' homework done?

And when asked to stop working
and wrestle
by errant 3-year-olds,
do razor moms stop
or only rarely?

Literature Cited

Halpern, D. (2005). Psychology at the intersection of work and family. *American Psychologist*, 60(5), 397-409.

Shriver, M. (2009). The Shriver Report: A woman's nation changes everything. Simon and Schuster: New York.

Nate Mitchell
(Father of Garrett, 4, and Cassandra, 1 week old)
DeDe Wohlfarth
(Mother of Zach, 9, Gabrielle, 8, Naomi, 8, and Quentin, 6)

Spalding University

A Transitional Journey

Before coming to higher education, I served as a teacher, principal, and Director of Staff Development for a large urban school district. I share this information because my experiences have fueled my research and writing. My first few published articles were written about initiatives that I created in my pk-12 life. In the graduate level classes that I teach I encourage our candidates to reflect and write about their practice. I encourage practitioners to write about what they know. Now as a tenured faculty member I try to link my service, teaching and research agenda.

I work in a Metropolitan University, and my department prepares administrators to serve within our pk-12 community. Our department mission is to "*develop effective, visionary, intellectual, moral leaders who can cause positive change in education.*" My current research agenda focuses on leadership and social justice; my research agenda enhances my teaching and encourages my service responsibilities. In other words, I have focused alignment throughout all aspects of my work.

Writers Group

Within our department we have formed a support group to encourage our research, writing, and eventual publishing. This collegial network allows an opportunity to discuss our work, to fine tune our skills, to work collaboratively, and to celebrate our successes. This "study group" opportunity is well documented by research as being a successful technique for adult learning.

Research Triangles

Research Triangles are formed to encourage faculty to work collaboratively in research groups, where we are encouraged to spend time with our colleagues in establishing research agendas. Within our department I work within a Research Triangle where we have established action research efforts within the area pk-12 schools; with this effort we not only support our own desire to research, we serve as external program evaluators for our local schools. This process, of course, serves as a win-win collaborative and enhances our desire as a department to support our local schools.

Mentoring/Coaching

I work in a small department, and each one of the faculty members has offered various levels of mentoring and coaching. We make a conscious effort to encourage each others' success and celebrate our accomplishments. The culture is professional, scholarly as well as warm, and welcoming. As colleagues we offer words of encouragement and advice. Our college has provided opportunities for anyone "new" to meet and work as a supportive team. This process has presented an opportunity to become socialized with our departmental colleagues and to assist with networking across disciplines.

Tips for first timers

- Establish a research agenda that is aligned to your work.
- Find theory and research that supports your research agenda.
- Review manuscript guidelines from journals that you enjoy reading, which includes journals that you receive through various professional memberships, as well as journals that support your research agenda.
- Be clear on who is the audience for whom the article is written.
- Start your manuscript with a "hook" to quickly gain the reader's interest.
- Be clear, explain any acronyms and terminology.
- Use strong literary tools.
- Write and re-write; the more you re-write your manuscript, the stronger it becomes.
- Be patient; it takes time from submission to acceptance to eventually having a published manuscript.
- Have a goal: for example, to submit one manuscript per semester.

Summary

As a faculty member with previous experience in pk-12 schools, I believe it is imperative to begin writing on what you know. Find a research agenda that supports your work and is aligned to your short and long term goals. It is important that new faculty flourish professionally and move successfully through the reappointment, promotion and tenure process. Programs designed to support faculty research can help to recruit, develop, and retain quality faculty members. This goal must be supported by uniquely crafted programs that are designed to provide orientation and faculty development for all faculty members. Providing opportunities for faculty members to work in collaborative study teams, networks, and support groups offers a venue for new faculty members to become acculturated within the world of academia. The opportunity to work within collaborative work teams also serve to reduce feelings of isolation. Mentors and coaches would further provide the support new faculty need to balance teaching, research, and service.

References

Blackwell, J. (1989). Mentoring: An action strategy for increasing minority faculty. *Academe*, 75 (5), 8-14.

Clark, S. (1998). Women faculty in community colleges: Investigating the mystery. *Community College Review*, 26 (3), 77-89.

Evanoski, P. (1988). The role of mentoring in higher education. *Community Review*, 8 (2), 22-27.

Tierney, W. (1997). Organizational socialization in higher education. *Journal of Higher Education*, 68 (1), 1-16.

Karen Hayes
University of Nebraska Omaha

Order with Flexibility

The successful publishing process for me involves order and flexibility. Just as the type of publication can vary, so can process. The publishing process that I have used successfully in the past for articles, research, reports, studies, or general papers includes idea generation, manuscript, preparation, revision, and manuscript placement. Regardless of publication type, I always address the process as a research issue.

The publishing process involves a due date, which can either be internal (personal) or external. Once the date is determined, I work backwards from that date to establish a start date. I also create progress dates that allow me to check progress and make necessary adjustments if necessary. I always plan for the unexpected. If everything goes as planned, great, but if the unexpected happens, I am not surprised. Unexpected obstacles or surprises during the process can become distracters which can affect overall quality of the document.

Idea Generation

Ideas are everywhere. Generating an idea can be as simple as observing and developing a question. Often, I start with a simple who, what, when, where, how, or why question or thought since I consider ideas and questions the same. One does not have to depart one's discipline to find an idea, but it can be a plus. I have discovered that relating one's discipline to another can be a motivating experience. Researching the connection between two or more disciplines is a great idea in and of itself. I think most would agree that research begins with a question and usually ends with a question. I look for ideas generated during the research process and write them down for future research for articles, studies, or papers.

Manuscripts

I follow accepted writing style guidelines during manuscript preparation. I prefer APA guidelines, but if a particular writing style is mandated, I always follow the stated guidelines. Following required guidelines is very important when responding to a call for papers request. The manuscript should be clear, follow a format, possess readability, and not be dull. I do research in a compartmental or component manner which allows for flexibility in the process.

Preparation

The first thing I do is develop a plan of action that includes a timeline, the research tools, and dates for progress reviews. I also decide early in the preparation phase the type of research methodology I will be using, keeping in mind that the idea generated will usually determine the type of research required. I build components as I proceed in the process, which allows me take advantage of my location and access to research tools at a given time.

Revision

Allowing for flexibility in the process also permits modifications to be adapted when needed. At periodic time intervals, I connect related components of supporting data and revise as necessary. Another basic time proven rule I use for proofing is: if it doesn't sound right, it isn't and needs to be changed.

Manuscript Placement

I use three methods in determining manuscript placement. One is a call for papers, another is a self-directed target publication, and the last one is one of pure networking, which is actually a combination of the first two. I have determined that the manuscript placement plays a defining role in the preparation and planning mode of research. Usually a call for papers will set forth requirements for a particular writing style and usually a specific or general topic area to be addressed.

The technique of maintaining an order while allowing for flexibility throughout the publishing process definitely works for me.

Tony Adams
Eastern Kentucky University

Pre-Writing

Now that some of our colleagues with records of scholarly accomplishment have joined the conversation through pointing out overall strategies they use in their scholarly plans, it's time to focus on specific steps in those plans (i.e., pre-writing, writing, and post-writing). Check out these valuable tips involving the scholarly process.

Perhaps no area in the publishing process presents more problems than that of pre-writing. Remember your Newtonian physics and its first law—a body at rest tends to remain at rest. So it is with scholarly writing or the lack thereof. Potential writers understand that energy must replace inertia, but they are confronted with so many issues demanding attention before the first computer key is struck that too often the effort just doesn't seem worth it.

As you'll see in the following tips, strategies exist that can help you create momentum that propels you toward publication.

Working with the IR Office: You Have A Friend In The Business

Many colleges and universities have an Office of Institutional Research (IR) or similarly-titled unit that does reporting, analysis, and research on behalf of the institution. While IR is often seen on campus primarily as the "keeper of the numbers," what many scholars and researchers may not know is that the IR office can often provide support services to help in conducting research and in writing for scholarly publication. In fact, many IR professionals are themselves active scholars and can help in many facets of scholarly research, particularly in the social sciences, education, business, and the health sciences, among others. Typically, the best times to approach an IR office regarding your scholarly research are in the late spring and summer terms. These times occur when the office's institutional reporting responsibilities are lighter than in the fall and early spring terms.

While not all IR offices are able to provide support in all of the areas discussed below, due to resource and staffing limitations or institutional policy, many are able to assist in the following five categories:

(1) *Research Design and Methodology:* It is beneficial to work with an expert in research design *before* the study is begun, as errors or shortcomings in design cannot be easily overcome in the data collection and analysis phases. IR staff can help the researcher to design an effective study, including selection of variables, data collection protocols, sample composition, and sampling methods. In addition, IR professionals may be able to help the researcher to develop more complex designs, such as mixed quantitative/qualitative methodologies.

(2) *Survey Development and Implementation:* The IR office can assist in developing and administering a wide variety of survey instruments. This service includes helping to develop the individual items and sequencing them in an instrument that maximizes response rates and validity of findings. In addition to assisting with surveys, many IR professionals possess expertise in conducting focus groups and in-depth interviews, and can assist in developing protocols for administering these kinds of instruments, as well as providing guidance in conducting the interviews themselves.

Of particular benefit to researchers, many IR offices have access to online survey software, such as Zoomerang® or Snap®. Depending upon available resources and license agreements, your survey may be able to be loaded into your institution's online survey software, and the survey can be conducted online via an e-mail invitation. You may also want to secure your own access to an online survey package, which can be at little or no cost, depending on the software and number of items and respondents. Online surveys can be an efficient way to collect and analyze data for your study, particularly when you have ready access to respondents' e-mail addresses. Online survey software packages often have advanced administration and data analysis features, including filtering, cross-tabulation, and branching of items. Reports can often be viewed in real time, and responses can be downloaded directly to Excel spreadsheets or statistical software, such as SPSS.

(3) *Statistical and Analytical Support:* IR professionals can help the researcher to select the appropriate statistical tests and analytical methods that best fit the purpose and design of the study. Most IR professionals have strong backgrounds in descriptive and inferential statistics, and many also have experience in areas such as predictive and causal modeling, data mining, forecasting, and the like. In addition to quantitative data analysis, IR staff can also assist the researcher in preparing to analyze qualitative data, such as content analysis for interviews and focus group results.

(4) *Access to Key Data:* Depending on institutional policies and resources, IR offices may be able to provide researchers with access to datasets, including summary student information, census information, survey responses, and the like. For example, many scholars have found particular benefit in pairing or merging summary student information such as retention/graduation rates or course-grade performance with data from

surveys such as the National Survey of Student Engagement (NSSE) or Cooperative Institutional Research Program (CIRP) Freshman Survey. IR offices can also help direct researchers to data resources from the U.S. Department of Education's National Center for Education Statistics (NCES), which provides a wealth of longitudinal information on virtually all aspects of higher education in the U.S. Particularly if the researcher has an interest in examining an aspect of the educational experience in his or her research, it may be beneficial to pay the IR office a visit to determine what kinds of information may be available, either on campus or beyond, to bring to bear on the question(s) at hand.

(5) *Boundary Spanner and Clearinghouse:* As noted above, IR is the keeper of many pieces of critical information at the institution. As such, it also serves as an important link or "boundary spanner" between and among departments and functions, particularly in critical aspects such as student retention. For example, IR can connect a department that has undertaken a successful retention initiative with a department searching for help in retention performance. Likewise, if IR has been working with researchers across the institution, it can help to connect active scholars in a particular area with those seeking to develop a research program in a similar area.

As discussed above, the IR office can help in a variety of ways to enhance the scholarly research capabilities of the institution and to make your research study as strong a candidate as possible for inclusion in your intended journal or outlet. A wealth of talent and experience resides in the IR office, and these resources are often overlooked when scholars conduct important research that benefits the institution, their departments, and their disciplines.

E. J. Keeley
Eastern Kentucky University

Indentifying Emerging Topics of Scholarly Interest in the Discipline

Over the past decade, the venues for presenting and publishing peer-reviewed scholarly work have increased significantly. The general criteria for acceptance of proposals and papers require that the document be of high quality, well written, novel, accurate, relevant, and at the cutting-edge of the discipline. Reviewers evaluating the submissions are eager for a glimpse of this unfolding future being ushered in by professionals in their respective disciplines. Contributing to the existing body of knowledge often requires finding new insights and applications of earlier work. In addition, interdisciplinary progress requires expanding the knowledge horizon in unconventional ways. Scholars can increase the odds of their presentations, papers, or research proposals being selected following the peer-review process by directing their efforts toward new trends or emerging topics identified as being of professional interest.

Identifying and developing ideas related to emerging areas within a broad field of study offer a promising opportunity for scholarly work. For example, conferences are often organized around emerging scholarly areas, and bring together professionals for sharing ideas related to specific topics. These topics may be highlighted as the central theme of a conference, such as "Green ...," or "Online ...," or "Global ...." They may also appear as explicit or implicit directions to potential contributors about the key areas in which proposals are being solicited for review. Areas of scholarly interest within a discipline are generally identified by different working groups within the association or organization, along with reviewers of different topical areas. In the absence of such directions, some detective work is needed to identify areas of future growth. These areas could be based on the interest shown by peers during conference presentations, professional meetings, or in the selection of papers accepted for publication in the conference proceedings from previous years. In addition, some conferences and journals or tracks may prefer qualitative work, and others purely quantitative work backed by rigorous analysis. A review of prior work accepted by the conference can offer a method of matching one's interests and expertise with the type of publication, and hence lessen the possibility of a mismatch. Since the development of a proposal takes a considerable amount of time and effort, any work done to increase the possibility of a successful match should be explored.

Reviewers pay careful attention to determine how closely the submitted work fits the theme of the conference or journal. This desired meld includes the topic, title, abstract, main ideas, results and conclusions, along with the methodology followed. Take time in selecting the topic as it will require a significant investment of time and resources. Topics outside the scope of the conference are likely to be cut as part of the review process. A title that that uses appropriate keywords can draw the attention of the reader and enable it to be picked up by bibliographic database searches. The abstract serves to draw the reader into the work and without a strong overview in this section, the other portions of the paper may not receive full attention. The relevance and applicability of the content to the user must be clearly presented in the abstract. Recognizing that academic works builds on the foundational ideas of scholars in the area, you should indicate how your particular work improves, expands or extends the original ideas. The novelty of the contribution should be highlighted, along with any practical applications that emphasize its usefulness. By the same token, the conclusions section of the work should summarize the results, pointing to their broader impact, and, if applicable, indicating directions of future work being investigated. The remainder of the document should, of course, hold up under the close scrutiny of the multiple reviewers, emphasizing the key contributions of the work. In almost all of our peer-reviewed presentation proposals that have been accepted over the past five years we have tried to: (a) stay within the stated theme of the conference organizers, and (b) base the presentation on the interest shown by participants during the prior conference or on the selection of papers in the conference proceedings.

A judicious selection of topics for development of peer-reviewed proposals or papers can also help balance faculty teaching and scholarly responsibilities. For developing programs, faculty members need to identify the latest trends and bring those high-quality and novel ideas into the classroom. At the same time professional associations are eager to hear about the instructional experiences of faculty members. By selecting topics that are related to the academic program goals and which also intersect emerging topics identified by the professional association, faculty can reduce duplication of work. Students also learn about the latest topics of interest to researchers in their disciplines and have the opportunity of contributing to its development. This strategy can be used to direct the scholarly efforts of faculty, and in doing so enhance the students' learning experience as well.

Vigs Chandra
Ray Richardson
Jeff Kilgore
Eastern Kentucky University

Differentiating Journals

Educators work tirelessly in academic pursuits, especially in preparing manuscripts for publication. Each manuscript is carefully scrutinized and evaluated. Frustration occurs after thought and wording are completed but the manuscript does not match the technical aspects of the journal to which the carefully orchestrated document is submitted. Attention to detail in planning can avoid these issues.

Many authors limit their initial planning to the task at hand, specifically the research, project, or writing process. At the beginning of a project, include some thought as to where the final product may be communicated. Your writing will be tailored in the technical format of the journal selected. Each journal will have "instructions for authors" which serve as a guide to formatting, length, sections, and citations. These instructions are outlined for use as your manuscript is created. The author's instruction guide is a tutorial for the format of the paper as well as a mechanism to preview article topics previously published by that journal.

A review of your target journal will help you decide if it is the right publication for your paper. Examine the journal for the types of manuscripts published. If the focus of the journal is consistently basic research, it probably is not the journal for your quality review paper. If a special themed edition has just been published regarding teaching methods, your paper about teaching methods probably will not be published too quickly as there is usually a gap of time before that theme is produced again. This is not to say that your paper will not be published by that journal. If your paper suggests a novel idea or new theory, the publisher may rush to print it. You might not know what themes are in the pipeline for circulation. The editor will inform you of a proposed theme edition in response to a letter of inquiry.

If you are uncertain as to which of a few journals to submit and each has its own formatting style, an investment in a software formatting program may be wise. Reference management software may be purchased, but there are also several excellent programs on line which can be downloaded to your computer without charge. These programs allow you to import citation information into a database which will then create a reference in the preferred format in your paper. Should your paper require modification to fit another publisher's formatting requirements, a simple change in the command to the software program will re-format your paper automatically. This will result in time savings and error reduction if you have to submit to several journals prior to finding an accepting publisher. The database of references can be stored and used by selecting individual entries at a later date in subsequent papers.

If authors' instructions are not presented or not clear, it is common practice to submit a manuscript draft double spaced with one inch margins. Indentations are preferred over an extra space between paragraphs. Right sided justification is not desired. Make sure you have proofread and spell-checked your document. References should be in the style of the journal to which you are submitting (Klausmeier, 2001). Typically 20-pound weight paper was used for the manuscript; however, today most documents are electronically submitted, which eliminates the need for the document to be on paper.

Selecting the journal for publication of your manuscript can be daunting. Knowledge of journals in your specialty area is probably well known. In every specialty there are journals that are considered superior while others tend to focus on a particular specialty area. Academics prefer to be published in the journal that rates highest in their academic setting. To find out which journal would be best in your specialty area, assess the journal's impact factor. Impact factors are calculated for all academic journals. This calculation is a statistic of how often articles are cited or referenced in future manuscripts. The theory is that the more a manuscript is cited, the more of a landmark article it is. Typically, a journal's articles will be tracked for two to three years. The number of citations of all of the published manuscripts for that journal is then averaged. This becomes the journal's impact factor or a measure of importance of the information contained in that journal (Garfield, 2006). Impact factors were originally calculated in science-related journals but are now being calculated for all journals. Journals with the highest impact factor generally focus on the latest and most rigorous research, promotion of theory, or radical shifts in processes. Novice writers will find a journal with a similar focus to their work to be the best journal of choice for publication of their work.

Submit to just one journal at a time. Publishers frown on authors who submit manuscripts to multiple journals at the same time. Editors desire to publish your work as a unique body of knowledge. They will work with you to improve your paper. Often peer reviewers provide their services for several journals. They will relate information that your manuscript has been reviewed for another journal and will check to make sure their suggestions were honored in subsequent submissions.

The technical aspects of publication vary by journal. With some preplanning and foresight, academic writers can meet the challenges up front and create an excellent presentation of their work.

References

Garfield, E. (2006). The history and meaning of the Journal Impact Factor. *Journal of the American Medical Association,* 295 (1), 90-93.

Klausmeier, H.J. (2001). Research writing in education and psychology-from planning to publication: A handbook. Charles C. Thomas Publisher, Springfield, IL, US.

Linda M. Schultz
Maryville University, St. Louis

How to Get Involved in Research

Jump right in....don't wait.

Identify your personal professional interests and passions - Start your personal research journey by identifying your personal passions connected to professional subjects and topics you are interested in or want to find out more about. Make sure that the research topic is in an area or specialty that you are intensely interested in as this will sustain your interest and encourage you to persevere with short and long term active participation with a research project.

Seek out experienced researchers with ongoing, active research projects - When you are just starting your research career, find an experienced mentor with ongoing projects in subject areas you are intensely interested in. Seek out seasoned researchers who are good teachers and interested in sharing their experience and expertise with you.

Join and actively participate in your local organizations - A good source for locating a mentor experienced in research, grant-writing and funding processes is your professional organization. Locate, join, and go to your local organizational meetings. This commitment is an excellent way to find out what is "happening"...not only in your local area but also on state-wide and national levels. Professional organizations frequently offer newsletters, listservs and online resources available to both members and nonmembers. Seed grants for faculty or employee development are frequently offered to beginning and established researchers in specific subjects and professional interests.

Take advantage of opportunities to learn skills - Research projects can offer excellent opportunities to learn grant writing skills information about where to find grant availability listings and announcements. There are numerous online resources in thousands of professional areas that offer grants ranging from a few hundred dollars to many thousands that sometimes are not awarded because no one applied.

Extra perks of your student role - If you are a full time undergraduate or graduate student or are enrolled in a continuing education program to maintain certification for career advancement or just to pursue additional interests, utilize academic internal and external resources to team up with an educational administrator or your dissertation chair on research projects. Offer your services to assist with a specific area of their research processes (i.e., literature review).

Locate internal and external research resources - Internal and external to your work environment research funding and development resources are generally available. Resources might include potential research partners in other departments or geographic areas within your organization. Statisticians can frequently be located within professional work environments. Statisticians play a very important role in all phases of a research project. Planning your statistical analysis at a very early stage in a research process is key to the ultimate ease of data analysis and the ability of your reporting and sharing your findings and ultimate article(s) publication in your professional organizations.

Star in a "minor" role - Starting as an assistant or a "key personel" due to your overall experience and/or experience in your specialty field is also a good pathway to starting or establishing your research "track record."

Jump in, start small, and build your research skills - with experienced mentors and you will be surprised how much you enjoy the once formidable process of "RESEARCH."

Wrennah L. Gabbert
Texas Tech University Health Science Center

Getting Started with Scholarly Writing

Don't be afraid! - Do not be afraid of "scholarly" writing. You can do it with practice and perseverance. However, you do need to know that there is both good news and bad news involved with the development of your writing skills. The bad news is that writing is hard work; the good news is that writing is a skill that can be learned and there are resources that can help you in gaining experience.

Choose a topic to write about that you are passionate about! - It is easier to get started in scholarly writing by choosing a topic you are passionate about and one you want to find out more about. Choosing an attractive subject will sustain your energy so you can devote the time and extra efforts required to persevere and complete your writing project. If the thought of choosing a topic you are passionate about leaves you completely lost, do a quick self-assessment by asking yourself the following questions: (1) What would I read about in my free time if I had unlimited access to magazines, newspapers, and all the libraries in the world? (2) What intrigues me professionally? and (3) What subject do I want to learn more about?

Squeezing time out of your busy schedule- Do not wait until you have time to write. If you wait until you have the time to write, you will never get started. Use small portions of time to start and develop your initial and expanded thoughts. As little as ten to fifteen minutes at a time can add up to a great deal of work. To find time to work on your writing skill acquisition, make an appointment with yourself so you can "steal" for your writing projects.

Build a Foundation - After identifying a subject you are passionate about, you will need to explore current, evidence-based resources. By accessing current resources, you not only find updated materials, but, at the same time, you will also be reading published examples of scholarly writing. While you are completing your literature review, you can practice your scholarly writing techniques by summarizing your findings for future reference.

Access to the world - Your literature review is easier than ever today with the online data bases available twenty-four hours a day that, quite literally, give you access to the "world" and extraordinary evidence-based, peer-reviewed substantive resources. While conducting your explorations you can simultaneously locate submission criteria and specific instructions regarding style, format, and length of articles for your completed project. Instructions for letters or emails of inquiry about your proposed topic can also be easily located during your journey through the vast world of resources you encounter.

Find a Mentor - To locate candidates you might consider for a mentor, ask yourself the following questions: (1) "Whose writing do I enjoy reading? (2) Is there someone I know at work or socially who writes well? and (3) Who do I know who is a published writer/has the same professional interests/has just completed an article?" After identifying potential candidates, call, email and/or make an appointment with them to discuss working with them on developing your scholarly writing skills. Offering to help them with their ongoing writing or research projects by helping with gathering resources that would contribute to the Literature Review for one of their ongoing or upcoming projects might be an excellent way to begin a mutually beneficial mentorship relationship. Many times when academic professionals find a kindred spirit who is passionate about similar topics and issues, they will more readily offer assistance and ultimately will want to co-author articles together. Working with your mentor and observing the submission and publication processes involved in getting scholarly work published is a valuable experience.

In Graduate School? - If you are in graduate school and looking for a "first" experience with scholarly writing, you might consider checking out the Editorial section in the professional publications that you read. The Letters to the Editor section in your field of expertise can be fertile ground for "practicing" and polishing your professional writing skills. Typically, journal editors are hungry for reality-based opinions from someone "in the trenches." Sharing successful procedures, policies and expert opinions in your professional journals not only provides valuable information for your colleagues but writing experience for you.

Share What YOU Know! - You have important information to share with your colleagues, especially those who are new to academia and the teaching profession. By sharing your expertise and experiences with your colleagues, you can also develop your scholarly writing skills through hard work, perseverance and practice!

Wrennah L. Gabbert
Texas Tech University Health Science Center

Writing Book Chapters for Publication

For many aspiring academics, obtaining high quality, peer-reviewed publications can mean the difference between the unemployment line and a tenure track position. For those who have already obtained an assistant professorship, publishing is a primary stepping stone to earning tenure. Regardless of one's standing or aspirations in academia, authoring and co-authoring textbook chapters can be an excellent and relatively easy way to attain peer-reviewed publications.

Many texts in numerous academic fields have senior editors. This situation means that the book has different authors for each chapter which are peer reviewed by the editor and the publisher, allowing for a variety of authors to write individual chapters for the book. The down side to publishing a chapter in a textbook is that the only individuals who get paid for their work are the editor and the publisher. However, the benefit to the contributing author is that he or she receives a publication without traditional data collection, IRB approval, or months of waiting to hear back from a professional journal. Additionally, if the textbook makes it to multiple editions, with a few updates every few years, the contributing authors are all but guaranteed multiple publications.

We would like to share three main strategies that are helpful in securing the opportunity to write book chapters. First, it is beneficial to choose several texts to which you would enjoy contributing. One strategy is to look through texts you often use to prepare lectures or research. Another strategy is to conduct a simple web, library, or publisher search. After you have selected several texts, read a number (if not all) of the chapters in each of the texts you have selected in order to familiarize yourself with the subjects covered as well as the format and writing style of the chapters.

Second, you must contact the editors of the texts and express your interest in submitting a chapter. Although you could try an e-mail or a letter to the editors, this tactic is not likely to garner you a chapter. In many cases, textbooks represent an ample piece of the editors' livelihoods, so it is unlikely that they are going to agree to include your chapter without meeting you in person. A phone call expressing your interest in authoring a chapter in their book may earn you a sit down "interview" of sorts with the editors in question. Most textbook editors only offer chapters to those individuals who have a genuine interest and expertise in their particular field. Editors are looking for individuals who already possess specialty knowledge and are likely to update the chapter every few years as the text goes through multiple editions. Editors are also likely to request a sample of your writing. If you are already published, provide them with a sample of what you consider to be your best work. If you are not published, provide them with a sample of your thesis, dissertation, or other high quality graduate paper.

Finally, once the editor has agreed to let you author one of the chapters, you must clarify the editor's expectations before writing. Asking the right questions early in the chapter-writing process will save both you and the editor a great deal of work in the long run. First, find out the deadline of the chapter. It is imperative that you don't just stick to the deadline, but send your draft to the editor up to two weeks early. Doing so will demonstrate your reliability as well as give the editor ample time to suggest changes to your chapter. If this is your first chapter or the first time working with a new editor, expect to write multiple drafts.

Second, before you begin writing, ask the editor for an outline or suggested headings for your chapter. Most editors use "templates" for their chapters which help to streamline the style of the chapters and expedite the publishing process. If the editor provides this template, do not deviate from the suggested outline without asking permission. In the unlikely event the editor does not provide you with an outline or suggested headings, ask him/her to "sign off" on an outline you create. Doing so will help you to avoid, "This is not what I asked for" or "I wanted you to cover different things" responses when you submit your chapter.

Keep in mind that publishing a book chapter is every bit as rigorous a process as publishing a research article, just in a different way. A book chapter is not something that you can sit down and write in just a couple of days. Rather, it is a time consuming process that requires hours of reading the current and historical literature on your subject. One strategy to assist in this process is to enlist the support of your students in the literature search. Learning to conduct a proper literature search and review is an important skill for those interested in graduate school or already in graduate training. Your students could gain an invaluable skill assisting in the project. However, if involving students in the actual writing process, you will need to ensure the writing is of the highest quality.

Writing an edited book chapter can be a challenging and highly rewarding process. For those in academia who have a love for writing, but have barriers to traditional data collection, book chapters can be a meaningful and impactful publication. Additionally, once the editor is impressed with your well-written book chapter, you will find yourself invited for later editions of the same text as well as having a published book chapter to offer as a writing sample to a different editor of another important book in your field.

Nathaniel G. Mitchell
Jonathan W. Carrier
Dede Wolfarth
Spalding University

Time: The Elusive Ingredient in a Successful Recipe

Where in blazes (OK, you fill in the appropriate word.) do I find the time to excel at this publishing game? Many researchers, from assistant to full professors, find themselves asking this question as they strive to meet the publishing requirements in today's universities. When one author directed the Sam Houston State University (SHSU) Across-the-University Writing Program several years ago, she invited Toby Fulwiler to be a guest speaker at a two-day, university-wide faculty retreat. Fulwiler posed the question to our faculty, "What makes writing hard?" Overwhelmingly, the response revolved around time. Many questioned, "Where do I find the time to do stellar research that is worthy of reading and to crank out publications, especially when the number required keeps increasing?" We've found a recipe.

Writers who have numerous books and articles published mention different recipes for success. Ken Henson, author of over twenty-five books and hundreds of articles, typically spends all Saturday mornings at his favorite coffee shop and writes until noon. By using this method, he's away from the phone, his e-mails, and other distractions. He then reserves Saturday nights for his ballroom dancing dates with his lovely wife. Taking Henson's tip to carve out time, one author devotes her hours on planes, sitting in airport terminals, and during conference lulls to writing. The other recently worked on this piece while attending jury duty.

Judy Olson exclaimed that James, her husband and a Pulitzer nominee in history, writes on napkins while waiting for his morning toast. He continually thinks of ideas and jots them down so that he won't forget. Along with being nominated for the Pulitzer by John Hopkins University Press, Olson has written over thirty books, and the *Los Angeles Times* recognized him as one of the best non-fiction writers in America. Henson and Olson have different writing styles, but they have found what works for them. That's a key ingredient. We all have varied approaches, and we have to discover our personal recipe. Today, one author is procrastinating by writing this article's draft rather than grading the seventy-five essay tests staring at her from across the room. Writing this piece is definitely more fun and rewarding. It's putting a puzzle together.

While in graduate school, one author's dissertation chair, Professor Emeritus Zenobia Verner, emphasized that all graduate students and faculty needed to have four manuscripts simultaneously moving—one sloshing around in their heads, one draft on the computer, one manuscript sent to reviewers, and one piece accepted for publication. By heeding this sage advice throughout her career, this author found what works for her. Another tip she uses is letting the draft linger for a couple of weeks. With fresh eyes, she sees the glaring holes and tweaks the words to make it stronger. A worthwhile piece is not typically finished in one, or ten sittings.

Without passion the recipe will flop. Do you, as an author, have something worthwhile to contribute that others will find intriguing? Does your article answer the "so what" factor? Would anyone care about what you are saying, or will three people read it once it's printed—the editor, your spouse, and you? Well, maybe not your spouse. If you're yearning to know more about the particular topic, you have probably had some experience that relates. For example, one author wrote her dissertation on department chairs because she was one, and she wanted to know what other chairs did. If you're making yourself write a piece, it's probably not what you need to be doing. If it's not running around in your head, you probably need to skip to a more suitable subject matter that captivates you. Writing about topics that you care about might take more time upfront, but those manuscripts will actually get published, so you save time in the long run.

Building a reputation for creating solid, well-written manuscripts will save countless hours. Too often beginning writers send potential publications to editors without checking the journals' guidelines, seeing what the themed-issue concerns, or following the correct bibliographical format. Editors and reviewers do not want to spend time reading manuscripts that will be rejected or that have so many flaws that it will take enormous rewrites. Revising the manuscript, reading it word-for-word backwards to check for spelling errors, considering where to rearrange paragraphs, double-checking the statistics in tables and graphs, will improve your manuscript immensely and keep you from having to paste your walls with rejection slips. Your time will be well spent by examining the piece methodically and making a name for yourself professionally. If you want to learn more about the publishing game and what makes writing good versus not-so-hot, volunteer to be a reviewer or editor. However, this is a trade-off because your quality time to write may evaporate.

During one author's thirty years in higher education, she has collaborated with numerous peers, and that technique has saved time. By working together, others have located sources, worked on bibliographies, analyzed research, and proofread manuscripts. Four, six, eight eyes are often better than two, and she can be working on several articles or books simultaneously. Part of the publishing game is quantitative.

Caution: You need to be the lead author on many publications, especially if you have contributed the most. Feelings sometimes get hurt if this decision is not made at the onset. Research what your university requires. While some administrators only count the first author listed (lead author), others give merit or promotions to everyone whose name appears on the publication. Still others only count refereed, blind peer-reviewed pieces. Several major educational journals, such as *Kappan* and *Educational Leadership*, have editorial staffs rather than using a peer-review process. Avoid wasting time on writing that will never be considered for promotion and tenure if those are your goals.

One problem to having collaborators is arranging schedules so that everyone can meet. Yes, conference calls, e-mails, blogs, wikis can all aid in solving this dilemma, yet it requires meeting in some form. Giving everyone a specific role to complete by a designated time makes the process run smoother. Who will find research to support the findings? Who will analyze the five hundred questionnaires and create the graphs? Both authors have been involved with writing groups that meet regularly to critique each other's writing and offer constructive feedback. For instance, at SHSU, faculty members interested in writing used to meet twice a month. A doctoral student/librarian working on her dissertation collected manuscripts from group members who wanted to share their materials. We critiqued the unpublished papers, including pieces from her dissertation, and offered comments during bi-monthly meetings. Because these comments were oftentimes positive and the feedback specific, writers felt comfortable sharing, and numerous publications evolved from these one-on-one-half hour sessions. Did it take time to attend the meetings? Yes. Did it save time in the long run? Yes!

This one author has now graded her students' essays and turned in final grades.

Several weeks have passed since she wrote the initial draft. Today, she spent several hours again rearranging paragraphs, selecting the perfect words, and making the writing come alive. It's now ready. We hope our recipe for success will aid you on your publication journey.

Patricia Williams
Andrea Foster
Sam Houston State University

When You Really Need it Published...

When asked the question "What Works for Me?" concerning getting published, I immediately think about the most important aspect of the writing process, the plan! The plan requires immense strategic thinking; thus, it's quite demanding. Whatever the type of publication that one may be pursuing, a book, a scholarly article, or a simple literary piece, a well contrived plan to achieve that goal is truly the primary ingredient. I will put forth in a very above-board manner what it will take to successfully publish an airtight plan. Of course, at this point, it is worth mentioning that my advice is directed at the writing process versus how to enhance one's writing style.

At the time I begin to pursue the noble notion of publishing, I first begin developing the plan by broadly thinking about areas that I passionately desire to affect. Yes, you read it correctly; passion drives the writing process. If you have ever attempted to publish and became weary during the process, you could attest to the fact that it is passion that keeps the engine humming along. Once the tank is topped-off with the fuel of passion, I begin my journey across the landscape of educational problems seeking to exit at that one problem in which there exists both an authentic and exigent need for a solution. As an education practitioner and faculty member for scores of years, I am aware of a plethora of these types of problems. Now, the critical work of peeling back the onion begins.

Generally speaking, I would identify key concepts about the topic and subsequently begin the exploratory process of discovering information both about the topic and ancillary key concepts. For example, if I discovered that a disproportionate percentage of Asian-American ninth grade students in the local school district are at-risk of failing introduction to Algebra, I would begin an exploration into substantiated general causes concerning the phenomenon. If the outcome of the investigation yielded both appropriate and sufficient solutions, the process would terminate at this point. Conversely, if the exploration did not yield appropriate and sufficient solutions, that becomes a green light for the research. Subsequently, I would draft a research plan with specific steps that would include a panoramic view of the problem and a systematic approach to problem-resolution, though the plan would be developed through-and-through with expert consultation with other professional educators.

The research plan would allow for the precise analysis of the problem step-by-step from multiple perspectives, such as an evaluation of distinctive attributes of instructional strategies, prevalence of teacher and student apathy, student locus of control, parental support, etc. Additionally, the research plan would include a searching out of established solutions and a systematic and systemic evaluation of innovative approaches. Once the research plan has been crafted, I would look for funding sources that would support my research plan. This step is truly where the rubber meets the road. After a funding source has been identified, the next step would be to complete the Request for Proposal in order to secure the funding. When the funding has been secured, I am able to implement the proposed research plan. Subsequent outcomes from the research project will result in written products that can be used to publish in a myriad of publication venues.

Generally speaking, publishing guidelines vary from publisher to publisher; therefore, at this juncture it is worth noting to first find a publisher and then to create the manuscript. Simply put, select a publisher first, and then write the manuscript! In regards to finding a publisher, I search for publishers at the local, state, national, and international levels who may have an interest in my research outcomes. Moreover, the key is to find a perfect fit matching the research project outcomes with the needs of the publisher, thus abating the need for seemingly incessant rewriting! I also check to see if the publisher has a notable reputation and if it is a refereed publication. Finally, I review the publication guidelines and deadlines to ensure that I have sufficient time to submit an appropriate manuscript.

Once I have reviewed the publication guidelines and deadlines, I next prepare my manuscript. Perhaps, this should be a fluid process because the manuscript is usually close to being written based upon the outcomes of the research project. As a rule, I write a thought-provoking introduction that will capture the interest of both the reader and the publisher. I try to remember that I only have one chance to make a first impression; thus, I make it terse and compelling! Next, I add the body of the paper, recommendations, and a very strong conclusion. Prior to submitting the manuscript, I usually push away from the writing of the manuscript for a couple of days, if time will permit, to garner a fresh perspective. Moreover, this step allows me to spot syntax errors and the like that typically take away from the quality of the manuscript. Additionally, it is well worth the time to have another colleague read through the manuscript and provide candid feedback.

Finally, after the review process has been completed, I submit the manuscript to the publisher. The manuscripts that I have submitted have been either accepted or accepted pending revisions. If the manuscript is accepted pending revisions, I quickly make revisions and resubmit it to the publisher. In conclusion, I have found that following a strategic plan coupled with a sound research plan has led to the publication of monographs, refereed journal articles, book chapters, case studies, and major grant awards.

Trinetia Respress
Tennessee State University

Writing

An old story is told about a Zen artist who is paid a large sum of money by a prince to paint the royal family crest, a fighting gamecock. After visiting the palace and viewing the bird, the artist retreats to the mountains. A year later he returns without the painting. When questioned by the prince about the painting, he once again observes the royal bird for a time before leaving. This process plays out again and again over five years. Finally, just as the prince is about to execute the artist for failure to fulfill his part of the bargain, the Zen master proclaims he is ready to paint. He approaches the canvas and with several quick strokes completes his painting in a matter of minutes. The shocked prince asks why the artist has taken five years, then spent less than five minutes in creation, to which the master replies, "The difficulty was in understanding the bird's essence; once that was achieved, rendering it on canvas was easy."

Now we won't claim that once you have mastered the pre-writing stage of the scholar's process, writing will be easy, but at least you're now ready to use some of the expert advice that follows to create pieces/research that give you a better chance at catching an editor's eye and achieving acceptance from peer reviewers.

Just don't take five years to create. P&T Committees have less patience than princes.

Free to Write: Capturing the Creative Flow

Academic writing can be an exhaustive process. In addition to innovative ideas and interpretation, knowledge of the field is essential. In the process of writing for publication, becoming mired in the mundane is all too easy, especially in searching for citations as the proverbial pen touches page. While having citations in academic publications is necessary, it needn't limit the creative writing process.

In order to maintain creative flow, I often find it beneficial to write and leave notations where citations will need to be added. For example, if I were to write "discrimination towards the obese is widespread in Western society," this statement would certainly need citations for validation. Even if I "knew" that discrimination existed, I would still need to cite this statement. If while in the creative mode, I were to stop writing to find several citations at that moment, the creative flow is likely to be stunted by the distraction, slowing the writing process (and achievement of a finished product) to a crawl. If instead I were to write "discrimination towards the obese is widespread in Western society (CITE)," I could then continue writing, leaving a reminder to later insert citations when in a less-creative mode.

Likewise, spending precious creative-time on formatting can serve as a distraction. Rather than spending time formatting charts, graphics, and fonts during the creative time, you can do formatting at other (less-creative) times. If there are several charts, format them all at the same time: at the end of the writing time, the end of creative-energy, or at the end of the project.

While adhering to these adjustments are small steps, they can save an author a lot of time, allowing the creative energy to flow rather than being stymied by non-critical distractions. Happy writing!

Leslie Elrod
University of Cincinnati

A Research/Scholarly Paper Outline

When I begin to do preliminary work related to starting a Research/Scholarly paper, I do what I ask my students to do for a term paper. Both have some similarities, but the professional research paper extends the process of investigation with the addition of several sections.

To begin, I think of a topic of interest that is broad and comprehensive. I then apply deductive thinking in an effort to narrow down the topic. Once I have a somewhat narrow topic of interest, I do some research on the topic. This broad research investigation looks at different aspects of my specific topic of interest, which leads to more deductive thinking to again narrow down to 5 to 10 articles that are connected with a similar thread.

After the initial research for related literature has been completed, the writing begins as well as the interpersonal learning. I take the task to teach myself about the topic in the manner of becoming an expert.

For a research paper the above is critical because of the importance of thoroughly knowing the area of interest. This knowledge leads directly to the "Introduction," which sets the stage for what is to follow in the paper. The **Introduction** is basically an overview of the full paper that covers the problem, the purpose, the type of survey that was conducted and the rationale for doing the research. An hypothesis is developed and introduced at this time.

The **Literature Review** brings a focus to the paper that connects existing studies to the area of interest. This section provides a clear conceptualization that either supports or refutes the subject. It is a good practice to include both supporting and non-supporting literature because at this stage the outcome is not known, but the research process will fall into either realm. Also in the Literature Review section a needs assessment is conducted to support the rationale for doing the research. If there is no need for the research because of the volume of information available on the topic, a different approach needs to be developed that addresses an aspect of the topic that is not fully developed. This section is written very much in a term paper format that looks at the problem, the existing literature, and the drawing of a conclusion.

The research paper, then, goes further with the addition of the **Methodology** section. In this section the evaluation design is fully developed so that anyone interested can duplicate the research. Close attention is necessary to cover a step-by-step description that walks the reader through each phase of the research project. The sampling procedure is a primary phase that gives a detailed view of how the subjects were obtained and interviewed. The subjects can be obtained from a random to a selective random sampling procedure. Then follows the method by which the data is collected, either from a survey or a person-to-person interview. Again, the importance of detail cannot be overstressed because of the previously mentioned possibility of duplication of the research project by someone who has a similar interest. Finally the instrument used to conduct the research is provided to give the reader a specific reference as to what was asked of each subject who participated in the research project.

The next section is the **Results,** and here one will enter the findings relative to the stated problem and the purpose of the overall study. Also, all statistical data and assessment will be reported in the Results section. The Results section is a clearly written account of the outcomes that utilizes possible graphs and tables to highlight the findings.

Following the Results is a reporting of the **Demographics,** which includes a general description of the respondents i.e., number of males and females, the age and overall average age, marital status, religion, the number who refused to participate, and a further description of any unique characteristics that surfaced. The Demographics section is also a written explanation that gives the reader a picture of the respondent population, and the use of possible graphs and tables is determined by the best method of presentation of the information.

The **Discussion** section can be considered the most enjoyable part of the paper because here is where the author gets to shine. The first component directly describes what the whole study means. This description includes an overview of the problem, the purpose, the rationale, and the hypothesis. The overview covers a great deal of what is in the Introduction but in a more defined manner. The second component involves a narrative on what was learned from doing the study. Here the author extrapolates from the statistical data and the findings to draw conclusions and possible trends. The third component is a statement that highlights the specific outcomes of the study. The final component provides the author the opportunity to give his/her impression of having done the study. At this point it is important to utilize inductive thinking to illustrate what the outcomes could lead to in the overall bigger picture.

The last section is the **Limitations,** and here is the time to reflect on all the elements of the study and discuss what could have been done or could be done to improve the study. This section is also the time to address the lessons learned from conducting the study, emphasizing those things that were unaccounted for during the planning and implementation phases. Finally, I provide the reader with recommendations that could lead to new research.

Throughout the process it is evident that one must be transparent in the description and writing of the research/scholarly paper. I follow the above outline when I begin a new research project, while I am in the process, and as I conclude my project.

Gary L. Villereal
Western Kentucky University

A Timely Trifecta

Organization and consistency are two key ingredients that help me to be productive with my scholarly work. I have found it imperative to write and research on a scheduled daily basis (as best I can), if only for a few minutes every day, than to try to find large blocks of time less frequently. To make sure I am consistent with my research writing, I have crafted a three-part plan that helps me schedule all my activities, especially my scholarly projects.

Yearly Plan

I start with my Yearly Plan. My Yearly Plan is an organizational chart divided into the fall, spring, and summer semesters. Each semester chart is divided into three columns with the first column noting due dates for all activities, the second column listing the activities and projects, while the third column is to check off project completion. I develop my chart by identifying in the second column all the projects for the new academic year, including research projects, major course work or curricular activities and revisions, and other major committee or organization activities. Then I identify the specific due dates in the first column, such as conference submission deadlines for presentation proposals, journal submission due dates or committee work deadlines for projects, which I can transfer to my calendar. When I complete a project, I get the satisfaction of checking it off in the third column. This timeline helps me to set the stage for the new academic year, assay my work load, and manipulate my calendar. I can easily view the kinds of work that will need to be accomplished and when, and decide what other projects I can commit to or not commit to. The timeline also helps to better balance my work life and personal life. I always make sure I have extra lines in the chart so that I add to and revise this chart as the school year progresses and as various activities evolve or dissolve from work with committees and organizations. I keep this Yearly Calendar posted at my desk, so it is visible and a constant reminder.

Research Accountability Calendar

My Research Accountability Calendar is my next tool of organization. The Research Accountability Calendar helps to keep track of the time I commit to my research each day of every month. This calendar is a three-column chart for each month of the year, beginning with September and ending with August. The first column is for the date, the next column is for the amount of time I work on research each day, and the third column is to briefly note what I accomplished, such as "reviewed articles," "revised introduction," or "worked with data." When I get this chart out every day to jot the amount of time I have worked, I feel guilty if I don't mark any time on my calendar, even if for 20 minutes. It truly makes me accountable to me. I keep the Research Accountability Calendar with my research projects on a flash drive so it goes with me everywhere.

Spiral Notebook

The third part of my organizational plan is the use of a separate spiral notebook for each research project. I keep a spiral notebook in which I may sketch a flow chart of ideas, list possible titles for articles, jot down potential journal titles, or other ideas that come to me as I am working on a project and don't want to lose those thoughts. I also list what I need to do to complete the project. When I finish my research work for the day, I note the date and briefly list the next steps that need to be done the next day. This process helps with continuity and keeps me heading in the right direction. The spiral notebook is extremely helpful if I have to miss a day or two of research writing; the "to do" list refreshes my memory and quickly gets me back on track.

We lead very busy lives researching and presenting our scholarly work along with teaching our courses, revising curriculum, working with students and participating in committee responsibilities, so being organized is one way I feel I can stay ahead of the game. I bet it will work for you!

Jan Walker
Drake University

Getting Down to the Real Work of Scholarly Writing

Steal Some Time – Don't wait until you have time to write. If you wait until you have time to write, you will never get started! Use small chunks of time between committee meetings, during your lunch break, or when "stuck" in a waiting room or airport. Get in the habit of carrying a way to record thoughts and ideas that come to you wherever you are. Do not worry about using a specific high tech format... use what YOU HAVE. Use a format you feel comfortable with, low tech (notepads, pens, pencils) or high tech (cell phone, voice recorder, laptop, pda, etc.). All formats can work equally well for documenting your ideas. Most important is to use a recording format that you can keep WITH you and have readily accessible to help you record your thoughts when they "come" to you.

Making your Notes Count – Record your thoughts and add a brief note so you can accurately describe, elaborate and expand them at your next "stolen" moment. From your initial notes make an outline of your main ideas and thoughts. If you have not explored the latest evidence-based information about your subject, you will want to consider doing so at this point because your next task is to expand on these main ideas in your outline. After completing your exploration of current resources, expand and elaborate on your thoughts in outline form by reinforcing your main points with your findings. Augment your thoughts and findings with personal experiences to provide greater depth with application and connections to real life and to give your article LIFE!

From Outline to Rough Draft – After completing and expanding your working outline, your next step is to start working on your rough draft. Taking your thoughts from an expanded outline format and turning them into a publication is a major portion of the hard work of scholarly writing. Creating your rough draft is time consuming and hard work because the process consists of writing, rewording, and rewriting until your sentences and paragraphs say what you want them to say in a professional, polished format. This process is not easy and takes time, practice, and patience.

Let it Sit – Revise, reword, and rework your rough draft until it conveys the message and intent you wish and then leave it alone for at least a few days if at all possible. Letting your writing "gel" for a few days is beneficial because you can come back with fresh eyes. Most of the time you will return to find areas that need to be revised. It is at this point that you should also revise for awkward, short, or choppy sentences. Read your rough draft out loud to catch any awkward sentences or verb tenses that are not consistent throughout your work. As you revise and polish your article, be sure and remember to insert any citations and references to avoid unintentional plagiarism. If you have a scholarly writing mentor, have him/her read your rough draft. Colleagues with expertise in your topic of interest can provide valuable feedback for content and format editing. Obtaining feedback from friends (outside your chosen professional field) can also give you valuable opinions about the readability and interest factor of your writing project.

The Homestretch – Congratulations! You have completed your article and submitted it to an appropriate professional journal! Hopefully, you will experience the pleasure of having your article accepted without any revisions or comments to be addressed. Frequently you will receive notice that your article needs revisions or has not been accepted "at this time" for publication. I urge you to view these occurrences as opportunities for continued growth and development of your writing skills. If your article is rejected outright, I urge you to contact the section editor and respectfully ask about the reasons your article did not fit their needs (if this information is not included in your rejection notice). Keep in mind the reason for rejection of your article could be because an entire journal was recently devoted to your topic and it is too soon for a repeat article on the same or similar topic. Inquire if there would be interest in your article at a later date. If writing style or format (APA, etc.) is an issue, ask about any resources they could recommend for neophyte scholars. Frequently, editors and other scholarly writers have encountered online resources or publications that can assist young writers with the development of their professional writing skills. If you are asked to complete revisions and given specific instructions on the areas to address, please follow the directions and return your article to the editor as soon as possible. Additionally, working with an experienced editor can provide a priceless opportunity for constructive criticism from an expert that will help you develop your writing skills. The ultimate reward for your hard work is in seeing your scholarly writing published and knowing that you are sharing your thoughts, expertise and experiences with a vast audience of your peers.

Remember – Do not be afraid of scholarly writing! It is important for you to share your work—professional and applicable life experiences—with your colleagues. You might save someone from making a tragic mistake, give that individual vital information in language he or she can understand, or share your passion about your chosen topic and "spark" interest, energy, and excitement in others. Scholarly Writing is a skill and can be learned, and YOU CAN learn how to share YOUR "real life" experiences through scholarly writing by practicing your writing skills, working hard, and persevering!

Wrennah L. Gabbert
Texas Tech University Health Science Center

Post-Writing

In the later years of his career, William Faulkner would walk to his mailbox every day in Oxford, pull out the envelopes, and hold them up to the sun. If he didn't spot a check within, he tossed them aside. Sometimes beginning scholars fall prey to the Faulkner Syndrome: if they receive a rejection slip for a submission, they discard their work, thinking all is lost.

What follows are some timely tips to help you through the post-writing and submission process, even suggesting some strategies for turning rejection into acceptance. Your reward might never be a sunlit check from a publisher, but credit from a peer-reviewed journal sure shines a positive light on you at promotion and tenure time.

For Improved Scholarship, Know Your Editor(s)

By definition, an *editor* is a person having managerial and sometimes policy-making responsibility for the editorial part of a publishing firm, a newspaper, magazine, journal, or textbook. However, there are different meanings for this term depending on the type of publication.

For example, most top scholarly journals have an Editor, Consulting Editors, and Associate Editors. Each of these positions has a different responsibility. When you first submit a scholarly manuscript to the Editor, this person checks the manuscript for style and format according to the Policy and Guidelines for the particular journal. Any manuscript not prepared exactly according to these guidelines will immediately be returned to the author without processing. If the manuscript meets the journal guidelines, it then goes to an Associate Editor for content checking and applicable scholarship that is the standard for the journal, and if it meets this journal standard, the Associate Editor will then send the manuscript out usually to two reviewers (authors) who have published recently in the journal. Get to know the scholarship of these recent authors who have published similar articles in the journal, for they most likely will review your manuscript and judge it based on their scholarship. These reviewers have three choices: (1) accept the manuscript as presented, (2) accept with revisions, or (3) reject the manuscript. If the manuscript is rejected, and you believe your scholarship to be credible and up to the journal standards, challenge the review with specifics. If challenged, many times the Editor will send the manuscript to one of the Consulting Editors for his/her comments. Again, for more effective scholarship, get to know your Consulting Editors and their areas of expertise. The best way to get to know all of these editors is at professional meetings—especially at informal gatherings, institutes, and workshops—where a lot of scholarship is developed and nurtured. Scholarly patience is also needed since the average journal article takes at least a year to get published in a top journal.

Textbook publishing is an entirely different type of scholarship. Most major publishing companies have a Vice President and Editor-in-Chief who directs the publishing of all of the company's products and is the principle policy-making executive. You will probably never come into contact with this person. The first person you most likely will meet is a textbook sales representative, who has a number of schools in his/her territory. If you have a product or ideas for a product, this sales representative will send your product or ideas to a Sponsoring Editor. The Sponsoring Editor will then send the product out to many colleagues at different schools who use a similar product. If the majority of these reviewers believe the product is new, unique, and will generate sales revenue, then a contract will be issued by the Sponsoring Editor and signed by the Editor-in-Chief. Once again, get to know your colleagues at professional meetings and discuss your ideas with them. This exchange is free and usually very productive. After the contract has been signed, your product will be turned over to a Developmental Editor. Get to know this person as a part of your family since you will be working with this editor 24/7 to meet all deadlines and contractual obligations. Once these standards are met, the final product will be turned over to a Production Editor who will take your project to its final fruition. Along the way, marketing Managers and Editors will also get involved. Patience is also the key here. As a "rule of thumb," the average college textbook takes 3-5 years to get published.

John Harley
Eastern Kentucky University

Submitting A Manuscript? Do The Homework!

Assuming all has gone well and the guidelines established by other authors in this book have been followed, a complete manuscript should now be nearly ready. Even if you have checked for accuracy, proper wording, citations, erroneous mathematical errors, etc., the manuscript may not be completely ready for submission to a publishing medium. Before you submit to a journal or other outlet that uses a peer-review or editor for publication, you may want to do a bit of "homework" prior to hitting send or sealing the envelope...homework that will greatly increase the chances of your manuscript being accepted for publication.

The obvious starting point is the selection of the proper journal or other outlet to which you send the manuscript. While it may seem common sense to some, selection of an appropriate journal for publication is where new authors commit an early error. Quite simply, to determine if a journal is appropriate for your manuscript, you must do some "homework" or scrutinize the appropriateness of the journal prior to sending the manuscript. Shockingly, this is the number one reason manuscripts receive early or instant rejections. This article includes some highlights a scholar may want to investigate to determine "goodness of fit" for the manuscript to the intended journal.

First, determine if the manuscript is appropriate. Review previous issues of the potential journal, perhaps over the past few years, to determine the type of articles that are typically published. Is this a journal for research only? Is your manuscript in the scope of the journal? Do you see similar articles or subjects published? Is there an annual special issue that is appropriate? If you are new to publishing as a scholar, you may want to elicit the comments from more experienced colleagues as to the appropriateness of your manuscript for a particular journal. In summary, based on a review of past issues, consider the question, "Will my article be a valued contribution to this journal?" If the honest and objective answer is "yes," then you likely have found the correct avenue for publication. If the answer is "no," do not waste any more time; keep looking for a more appropriate venue.

Second, prior to submission of the manuscript, look for guidelines or recommendations from the journal or the editor regarding submissions. Some technical journals require very specific formats, and those submissions lacking the format may be instantly rejected. Other journals may prefer certain publication styles; if so, be sure to adapt your manuscript to the preferred style. Other requirements may include a need for multiple copies, removal of author's name, use of passive voice, prescribed fonts or type size, and double spacing. Whatever the guidelines suggest, make sure your manuscript is in compliance.

And third, give the manuscript a final review to ensure it makes a good first impression on the editor and reviewers. This review may be done by eliciting the assistance of a published colleague to provide comments or an entity on campus such as a writing center. The use of an outside, third party reader is invaluable. No matter how good the author may be, after the author's viewing the same manuscript over and over, some errors become invisible to the author but obvious to an external reviewer. In addition, it may be necessary to rework portions of the manuscript to better match the style of the intended journal. For example, if the journal typically uses headings such as introduction, conclusion, recommendations, the manuscript needs to be adjusted accordingly. Above all, make sure the manuscript addresses the audience of the journal in a proper manner.

Other pre-submission considerations exist, including looking into the circulation, acceptance rate, general visibility and turn-a-round time of a journal. The time between the submission of an article and a notification of rejection or acceptance can often be measured in months, which may seem more like years to a scholar new to publishing.

After receiving the manuscript, many editors will send out a notification of receipt. This only acknowledges your article was received and has no bearing whatsoever on possible publication. Because many editors volunteer their time for the progression of the field, it may be days before a manuscript is assessed to determine whether or not it may be appropriate for the journal. If the "homework" about the journal was conduced properly, the author should not worry about rejection at this point. Assuming the journal is peer reviewed, eventually the editor will distribute the manuscript to other peers in the field for blind review. In this process each reviewer will apply his/her subject matter expertise to the concepts, ideas, and/or findings in the manuscript and edit as appropriate. This process takes time, but a rule of thumb is if four months have passed and no contact has been made regarding the manuscript, it would be appropriate to contact the editor.

In summary, selection of the correct journal and following the submission guidelines for the journal are critical steps in the publishing process. While an individual manuscript may be outstanding, if it does not comply with the theme, audience, and purpose of a specific journal, it may be rejected without being sent out for further review. Also, many editors are volunteers with full-time careers. Following the submission guidelines to the letter makes their job easier and increases the chance the manuscript will be considered. And finally, if the "homework" is completed properly, the chances for an outright rejection will be greatly reduced.

Ray Richardson
Eastern Kentucky University

Applying Wagnerian Opera Theory to Scholarship: It Isn't Over Till...

Many of us develop a feeling of excitement when an email arrives from a journal editor to whom we have submitted a research article. Before we begin to read, we wonder, will it be rejection? We hope to be able to scratch this one off the list as "published." For those of us growing closer to tenure, we are eager to substantiate our portfolios. For others, the email could mean the difference in an "Associate" and "Full" Professorship. We begin to read and catch sight of those anticipated words, "We are pleased to inform you that your paper was enthusiastically received by our peer reviewers and editors and has been conditionally accepted for publication pending minor revisions."

As the excitement starts to fade, we recognize it is time to embark on the process of final revision and begin reading thoroughly the reviewers' comments. We execute exactly what we believe is requested. We read and reread our revisions and solicit friends and colleagues to scrutinize for us. We soon find ourselves, once again, staring at the monitor, with everything complete except the push of one button on the keyboard to resubmit our work. Click.

I previously heard a colleague claim, "Once you receive the email asking for revisions, you are in. It's pretty much a published article." Unfortunately, I took this a bit too literally, and after receiving a request for revisions email from an editor, quickly and quite negligently added a few details and resubmitted without giving it another thought. A few days later I received a reply email from the editor. It went something like this: "Your revised copy has been received back from our reviewers. The recommendation is not to publish this article at this time. Some reviewers have written comments which you may want to address (see PDF attachment). We recognize that writing is hard work and appreciate your submission to the Journal."

I read it again. I suddenly realized that I had basically thrown away the opportunity to publish an article in a well-established and reputable journal all because I had developed a quite arrogant attitude. I began to feel annoyance at my irresponsibility and supercilious disposition. I finally decided that it had been a good but costly lesson and filed the email and article for future submission to a different journal.

After days of contemplating this experience, I revisited the peer reviewers' suggestions and began to rework the article with more "intelligibility" than the initial go around. Once the more precise revisions were complete, I began to search for a new journal to which to submit the article. Finding the right journal is a key to acquiring publication of your manuscript, and I was having difficulty detecting a suitable format for the topic of my article.

With some hesitation, I decided to appeal to the editor of the initial journal where the article was submitted in hopes that I would be granted another chance. My email went as follows: "I would like to resubmit the article previously returned for revision then rejected. This was totally my fault as I rushed through the revisions. I apologize and would appreciate another chance possibly for publication in the fall edition. I have attached the revised article and cover letter. Thank you for your consideration."

Fortunately, the editors did not hold the earlier blunder against me and gave me a second chance. My article was accepted and published in the next edition.

Never think that just because an editor asks for revisions, and even perhaps states that pending revisions he/she would like to publish an article, that the article is automatically accepted. You should always convey your best work in your first submission. If the reviewers request revisions, execute your absolute best the first time, and if, after revisions, the article is ultimately rejected, it cannot hurt to rework the manuscript and petition for one more chance. Like Brunhilda singing *Twilight of the Gods,* and that old saying, "It isn't over till the fat lady sings," a manuscript isn't published till it's published.

Greta Freeman
University of South Carolina Upstate

Turning Rejection Letters Into Positive Advice

Rejections are good for aspiring academic writers. The rejection letter is a reality check and a sober reminder that they still have some additional fine tuning to do. The positive approach to dealing with rejection letters is to look for the advice. In other words, take the comments, if there are any, and rewrite, rewrite, rewrite—this exercise gives you an opportunity to buff and polish a rejected piece of writing into an accepted piece of writing. There are three thoughts that I have about rejection letters.

First, remember that you are the writer, the creator, the engineer of your own work. Take control of what you produce. Focus your attention on the purpose of your writing project and then re-engineer your writing sample to reflect what the publisher is looking for. Let go and let your authentic self recreate the message you are aiming for in a manner which will impress the publisher. Again, remember, you are the creator of your works. Develop an ego and keep it!

Second, remember that you are not the only one to receive rejection letters. Some famous authors have received rejection after rejection. The rejection letter is one of the steps in being an academic author—it is part of the publishing process. How you handle rejection will determine how serious you are with your writing.

My third thought is simple: keep in mind that rejection can be a great motivator, a second chance to get it right.

The following are some of my strategies for overcoming the disappointment of receiving rejection letters.
- Don't stop writing. You must keep the momentum; keep your attention and mind focused on writing.
- Writing must become a habit. The rejection process must be understood as one step

in getting your writing off to a better start. Take time to lament, scream out loud if you must; but write all of the time. The volume of writing you do will give you much needed practice, and practice will inevitably give you a better chance of having your works accepted.

- Think of rejection letters as the voices of your private writing consultants. Listen to the advice of the publisher; however, don't forget that sometimes publishers are biased and their needs may be profit centered. If your rejection letter contains recommendations for improving your manuscript, then you have hit gold—incorporate the recommendations. Rewrite with the goal of improving your initial submission. Use the publisher's feedback to improve your writing project.
- Do not get frustrated, get even. When it comes to addressing rejections, fight the good fight. Talk with a talented writer and ask for advice. Listen to the experienced voice and incorporate valuable suggestions into your manuscript.
- Take the rejection as an invitation to stroll through the park, dine out, or attend a favorite movie. Pause for a moment and do something good for yourself. Writers are aware that they all too often have to make sacrifices in order to produce good writing. So, when that rejection letter arrives, view it as a golden opportunity to do something for yourself, shift gears for a moment, then get back to work.
- Put on your protective armor; don't let the pain of rejection hurt you. Just be prepared--have patience and thick skin. Psychologically, donning your armor gives you a sense of having some protection from the "enemy." That language may be a little harsh, but getting rejection letters is not a laughing matter, especially if you are a tenure track faculty member.

My mentor once told me to be tenacious about writing. When rejections come, and they will, I was advised to be steadfast in my efforts to refine my manuscript and get a fresh copy back to the editor. Do not give up! Work with conviction, be passionate, and keep producing new and fresh writing projects.

A final word about the rejection letters: I receive negative and positive rejection letters from editors. The positive ones provide sound advice; they recognize my potential as a writer. The positive rejections are more personal in tone. They show understanding, and, in some cases, they show empathy. Do not be discouraged; continue to aim for successful, published works. The following is an example of a positive rejection letter I received:

> Dear Sherwood:
>
> My apologies for the very long delay in getting back to you. . . I had hoped to carve but the time to not just read the material you sent, but to think about the cohesiveness of the project, and consider it in the light of the literature — but kept getting waylaid by issues that needed immediate attention.

> I've now found time to test my first impressions, and regret to say that, as it stands, I don't think the book will work. The chapters cover too much disparate ground: the experiences of both undergraduate and graduate students, faculty / classroom issues, student affairs, study abroad, and campus-wide diversity initiatives. I don't think there's enough material in any one area to make this a compelling purchase for a faculty member, a student affairs practitioner, or a diversity officer.
>
> I can see that the book reflects the wide variety of responsibilities that you have taken on, and the expertise you have developed, but regret that I feel the book needs a clearer focus on a defined audience. As it stands, I believe it would be hard to sell, Stylus Publishing, LLC / Kumarian Press (2010).

The fact that the publisher took the opportunity to read my manuscript and provide some thoughtful comments was greatly appreciated. I have taken time to digest the publisher's comments, and I am now in the process of re-thinking the overall project. In fact, I have decided to construct three manuscripts out of the one submitted. Now, how's that for thinking positively about rejection?

Reference

Stylus Publishing, LLC (2010). Sterling, VA.

Sherwood Thompson
Eastern Kentucky University

Other Scholarly Matters

Complementary to the pre-writing, writing, and post-writing stages are a few considerations that can serve to plant your feet more firmly in the scholarly world. Check out the following tips on sharing your scholarly experience with colleagues and students. Collaborating, mentoring, and just plain interacting with others offer ample rewards.

Collabowriting your Scholarship

Question I: what do the following works have in common? The King James *Bible*, the *Federalist Papers*, *The Pirates of Penzance*, and *Grimms' Fairy Tales*? Obviously they were all successful collaborations in some very different fields.

Question II: in the past twenty years, have collaborations in published scientific papers increased or decreased in terms of the number of their authors? Up ... in fact, one estimate claims the number of collaborators has doubled from six to twelve.

Question III: are the three of us qualified to muse upon collaborative scholarship? If you've been paying attention, you know Hal and Charlie have collaborated on over 800 items, but you probably didn't know that the three of us have worked together on articles, presentations, course creations, and even in writing communities.

What do we mean by collaborative scholarship? Friend & Cook (1990) claim the definition is "a partnership of equals working in a collegial and interdependent manner." We disagree in part. No partnership, even a long-lasting marriage, is ever between equals. Some people are just better at some things. Hal, for instance, is known as Dr. Grammar, Charlie is the right-brain best at coming up with new ideas, and Bill has an uncanny way of getting us together to produce. John-Steiner (1998) is much more elaborate: "The principles in true collaboration represent complementary domains of expertise ... they not only plan, decide, and act jointly, they also think together, combining independent conceptual schemes to create original frameworks ... there is a commitment to shared resources, power, and talent; no individual's point of view dominates, authority for decisions and actions resides in the group, and work products reflect a blending of all participants' contributions." Much better.

But, in truth, a range of collaboration exists. We know of two mystery writers who would rent a cabin, then take turns going upstairs to write alternate chapters of a novel on a typewriter. Tag-team writers. On the other hand, the three of us tend to collaborate on almost every step of the way from idea, to first draft, to revision. Total team collabowriting. Somewhere in between these poles lie most partnerships.

What types of collaborations are available? Three configurations stand out, though within each configuration sub-types exist:
- Faculty-Faculty (among peers, junior-senior)
- Faculty-Student (most often with grad students, but effective with juniors and seniors). Interestingly, the AACU recommends this collaboration as one of its best practices.
- Faculty-Administrator or Faculty-Staff.

Some of these partnerships fall under the category of mentoring, but in truth aren't all of them mentoring situations? And isn't it possible to be simultaneously the mentor and mentee?

Why should you collaborate? With apologies to David Letterman, here are our
Top Ten Reasons to Collabowrite:
- **Increase your ideation levels.** Research we found twenty-five years ago suggested a 60-70% increase was possible, but back then brainstorming was less respected than it is now. Last year we ran across an article in *Business Week* that suggested with three or more collaborators, the rate could be 400-700%. Three heads are better than one.
- **Mentor new faculty.** As the promotion, tenure, and evaluation process becomes more difficult and the scholarship bar is raised, new faculty need experienced faculty to guide them. Importantly, as accountability grows and teaching assumes more importance at institutions, new faculty need to be helped to see how scholarship can lift them up to where they belong in faculty ranks ("where the eagles fly," as the old song says), not become an albatross around their necks.
- **Use others' strengths to compensate for your weaknesses.** Most of us can excel at some things, but not all. Sometimes a partnership, as with Hal and Charlie, is more of a left brain-right brain merger. Other times, Hal and Charlie's lack of experience in educational research, especially the growing field of the Scholarship of Teaching and Learning (SOTL), needs the helping hand of a Master Po figure such as Bill. Other times it's not methodology, but area expertise. When Hal and Charlie started an article on daily assessment, they realized very quickly they needed the help of a colleague from the campus Office of Institutional Effectiveness.
- **Writing collaborated-upon pieces sharpens your communication skills.** When you write alone, you are fairly confident in what you mean, but the second someone else looks at what you've written, s/he may read it in an entirely different way. It's better to

have a co-writer question what you are trying to say than to have an editor reject your 30 pages because the piece was ambiguous. Sometimes a writing partner can show you an overall approach to an article, and sometimes it's just how to start one. Other times another writer can help you decide how much evidence is actually needed and whether one source is better than another. The very act of negotiating what you have written, arguing for or against something, helps. And just hearing someone else read what you have written can sometimes put your words in a different light. If nothing else, our vocabulary has increased over the years as well as our ability to utilize academic buzz words (e.g., inclusivity, accountability, foster ownership).

- **Increase your productivity levels.** For years one business metric has been production levels, and now that scholarship at most universities is assessed against a rubric, quantity is underscored (as in, for instance, the one-book standard or three peer-reviewed articles). The truth is that at most universities, whether they are research-oriented or regional comprehensives, the level of regularly produced scholarship is fairly low. In fact, Boice put that production rate at about 15% of the faculty.
- **Generate enthusiasm.** Yes, each of us working alone on a project has at some time become enthused at what we are doing. But if three or more of you are working on the same project, your odds of one of you being openly pleased on several occasions just went up. Enthusiasm, as we all know, is contagious, and its energy helps sustain the sometimes seemingly bland subjects (e.g., salt licks in Bullitt County history) that scholars find themselves working on. Isn't there a law of scholarship that finds the amount of enthusiasm necessary in direct proportion to the length of an article?
- **Become more sociable.** When we first arrived at Eastern Kentucky, nearly every faculty member took some time in the morning to visit the Faculty Club for strong coffee and conversation. Now we sit alone in our offices responding to emails and finding ourselves unable to match a face to the email signature. Even online teaching has detracted from the human element. We realize that some people collaborate over long distance through email, but we tend to get together daily when we're writing a piece.
- **Break down those silos.** Back in our Faculty Lounge days, George would tell us what was going on in history, and Klaus would elaborate on trends in poly sci. We would use each other for expertise and political perspective. Knowing each other, we would invite each other into the classroom. If Charlie was teaching the Federalist papers, he could probably get Bob from history to drop in for a guest lecture. Since those days, the revised Bloom's Pyramid has placed creating on top, but we as a university don't synthesize as well as we used to.
- **Model the collaborative process for your students.** If American business believes the number-one skill we can teach our students is team-work, what better way than to show them us doing it? When we place our students in groups, is our understanding

of their learning dynamic based on theory, personal experience, or both? We can read an article that talks about the necessity of student groups having assigned roles, for example, but until we have lived a partnership, we don't have the sense that those assigned roles really ought to rotate. Have you ever had a student in a group complain that "I do more than everyone else"? Actually, when you collaborate, you internalize and realize that it's important that you try to do 51% of the work with two and 34% with three and so on.

- **Writing and researching together prepares you for other types of academic collaboration.** Sooner or later you will be put on a committee and told the importance of service. The better you can accomplish this task, the greater your chances for success at that goal and personal advancement. Moreover, other forms of collaboration are becoming more important. Among the three of us, we are currently supervising (and sometimes facilitating) professional learning communities (PLC). One of the things we insist upon in a PLC is a work product, such as a presentation or publication. PLC members become better collaborators, and collaborating scholars become better PLC members. Learning to collaborate on scholarship also leads to team-teaching as well as to creating cross-disciplinary courses.

Will collaborative scholarship work for everyone? No, since some subjects are probably best explored by one person, especially if that subject/theory is one where the researcher is a pronounced expert and a lot farther down the road. Honestly, we have seen more collaborations, especially among students, fail than we have seen succeed, but that may have to do more with maturity and lower practice levels. Back to Letterman—here are our **Top Ten Problems with Collaboration:**

- **Promotion, tenure, and evaluation committees don't see a lot of collaborations,** and thus often they, and even their departmental guidelines—especially away from the sciences—don't know how to handle partnerships. In the sciences, for instance, the first-listed name on the research is the principal investigator (PI), but in the arts the listing might be alphabetical, by seniority, random, or attempt to reflect the amount of effort each succeeding participant put into the work; the problem is that no conventions exist at the moment. Some departments without much experience tend to weight the scholarship such that if three collaborators are listed, each receives one-third credit (we had this decimation occur early in our careers).
- **Collaboration is respected more in the sciences (hard and social) than in the arts.** Maybe it is the perceived history of the two scientists (e.g., the Curies, Bell and Watson) versus the distrust of two artists trying to work together a la Addison and Steele.
- **Junior colleagues often feel overpowered by senior colleagues,** or to state this insight another way, senior colleagues often "use" junior colleagues to do the work they (seniors) do not want to do, such as reviewing the literature (we know this term means something else to English professors) or constructing the Works Cited page. On the

other hand, some argue that this "using" is a time-honored rite of passage on the road to seniority.

- **Collaboration may not align with a university's or unit's strategic plan.** In an age of accountability, if something cannot be checked off as a key performance indicator of goals and strategic directions, it may not be recognized. Sometimes even if it is recognized, it is not credited (e.g., Hal and Charlie team-taught for over 30 years, but never received official credit for so doing; their effort was not financially rewarded or ever even given a load reduction). Or as an administrator told us, "If it can't be assessed, it doesn't exist!"
- **Collaboration runs counter to academic tradition and heritage.** When we think of great teachers, we tend to think of them as individuals. Robin Williams heading up the Dead Poets Society, Mr. Chips, Mr. Novak, Lucas Tanner. If you ever had a team-taught seminar, can you name your professors? Higher education focuses on the individual; you are hired into a single line, given an Employee Identification Number (EIN), and evaluated as a single entity (yes, we know shared positions exist, but each share is still evaluated separately).
- **Higher education is competitive.** Not all who are hired as assistant professors achieve tenure. The evaluation process is Darwinian where only the strong ... and accomplished ... survive. When faculty members collaborate, those same survival instincts sometimes take over. We came up in an era where the first grad student to find the key article in the library might razor it out of the journal so that all others would fail. Faculty still have been known to plagiarize, cut people out of grants, undercut them behind their backs, and generally look out for number one.
- **Collaborators are most comfortable with faculty who mirror their ideas.** On the other hand, what a good collaboration needs is opposition. When Hal and Charlie do carpentry work, Hal is constantly asking do we really want a joint here, a cut there, or to use nails? Hegel liked the thesis, antithesis, synthesis method of moving forward, and poet William Blake once said, "Without contraries is no progression." Good collaborators want to be led down the road not taken and shown what could happen in that yellow wood.
- **Collaborators must deal with conflict.** When each collaborator gets a few strides down those diverging roads, differences of opinion develop. Do faculty members have the ability to successfully negotiate this gap? Does the fact that the lectern is a bully pulpit impede their progress? Have departmental meetings and committee work prepared them sufficiently to deal with strong opinions? On the other hand, when you feel you are an expert of subject X (not a member of a university task force looking into alcohol and student housing problems), oppositional opinions are more difficult to accept.

- **Collaborators must carry their part of the load and produce.** You're feeling sick and call off class, and most students welcome the day off, but call off a meeting where your collaborator has spent hours researching, writing, and revising his/her section, and you have problems. That article you've been writing can reside in your computer for years, and you can keep telling yourself that you'll get to it soon, but you cannot lie or rationalize to fellow scholars who depend upon your timely production.
- **Collaborators must share.** Sometimes that is just a file or an email or that arcane bit of information you found after searching all Sunday afternoon while missing three football games. Some faculty can lend out their toys and some play best alone.

Let's suppose you've drunk the collaboratively mixed Kool-Aid our stand has been peddling, and you really want to try to produce some scholarly research. Well, here are some tips (too many to reduce to Letterman-size) to make that collaboration more effective:

- **Find collaborators you respect**, either as a person, an expert, or a willing experimenter with partnerships.
- **Try the market analysis approach** (which we've already explained).
- **Try to establish your roles early** (e.g., typist, background researcher, secretary, PI), but be willing to shift roles in the process.
- **Lose your ego.** Ideally when you complete your product, you have lost track of who contributed what.
- **Establish goals along the way.** Once you have the major goal defined, (e.g., a paper, a campus presentation, an article in a top-tier journal), set up secondary goals along the way (e.g., we want all the research completed in two weeks; we want a first draft by the end of the semester).
- **Keep a log.** Date your research and drafts. Note when you met.
- **Take time to reflect.** Just reading through your dates and logs will give you insight into your process, your progress, and your personalities.
- **Take responsibility for your assigned tasks.** Not only complete your task, but get it done early because something else "more important" will come along.
- **Focus more on your goals than having a good time.** A good time is what results from an effective partnership. If you find the good time taking primacy, maybe you should switch from scholarship to a social club.
- **Listen to what your collaborators say.** You may not like their ideas, but be professional enough to hear them out and then offer your opinion.
- **Let all ideas and suggestions live initially.** Don't be a killjoy. Often, a very offhand remark or marginal notation might be the key to making your collaboration outstanding. Down the road you can reject something.

- **Learn to piggyback.** These methods are classic techniques of brainstorming. David Kord Murray recently wrote a masterpiece called *Borrowing Brilliance* wherein he demonstrated how many theories and inventions have occurred because someone built on a predecessor's idea.
- **Finish the collaboration.** Former NFL commentator John Madden used to exhort offensive players to "finish the play"—i.e., gain as much yardage after contact as you can. In the same vein, we urge you to finish a collaboration. Even if it's unsuccessful, you will learn something. Almost anything you have produced is salvage-able, though perhaps in a different combination.

Hal Blythe
Charlie Sweet
Bill Phillips
Eastern Kentucky University

Listen And Learn

Sometimes the hardest part of writing is just getting started. Moving from the public school environment into the university is a tremendous, positive career change. However, the university's expectation for professors to publish poses a significant challenge for many new professors. I was one who struggled with this necessary task, perceiving writing as a bother. Frequently I muttered things like "I can't" or "I don't want to," thinking someone might jump in, tell me that writing for publication was just a trick, and then take me off the hook!

Instead, several of my colleagues swooped in with a very different message. Everywhere I turned, I found professors who had published, and I heard them speak of their work with a sense of accomplishment. Through ongoing dialogue, I found that the faculty was also prepared and willing to coach me as I began the process. They modeled collaboration and helped me see value in writing. Clearly, my success has been a result of numerous coworkers who motivated me and provided encouragement along the way. Finding a support system of experienced people is vitally important at the beginning of the writing process.

I can distinctly remember six faculty members who rescued me from the fear of writing and guided me to success. The first person was a professor who was brutally honest and basically told me to "get over it." I needed this push to move forward. This colleague became an ongoing encourager, helping me brainstorm topics and identify my passions and expertise to share with others. Every time I saw her, she would ask the question: "How are you coming with your writing?"

Another professor suggested that I begin writing by working jointly with another person. Luckily, she was willing to partner with me on a project in which we were both highly engaged. Her guidance was focused on setting a timeline and sticking to it. We discussed the different aspects of the paper that needed exploration and then framed them into a calendar. She served as our time-watcher, making sure we completed each step on schedule.

A third person who assisted me was an English teacher. She offered to proofread my work for grammar issues. She asked questions about the content, letting me know when information was vague or wordy. She recommended that I read my work aloud to hear the wording and any repetition.

When I quit procrastinating and buckled down to work, I found the courage to ask a prolific, respected writer to give me some helpful pointers. Her advice was of tremendous benefit. First, look at journals to find their upcoming themes and select ones that match my strengths and interests. She also told me to read articles from these journals to get the "flavor" of what appeals to editors and readers. The most explicit direction was to submit. As she pointed out, no one gets published by holding back work. You have to put something in the pipeline to reach your goal.

My fifth helper attended one of my presentations and suggested that I turn it into an article. In fact, he showed me how to break it into chunks and put it in an organized format. My creating an outline made the writing come easier. Once I had the roadmap of what I wanted to say, writing became more like having a conversation with another professional. He also suggested that I ask my students for feedback. I have taken drafts of papers to class and used them as springboards for discussion and critique. The feedback has been invaluable, providing details that strengthened the article by adding new and creative ideas, relevant examples, or more concise, direct language.

Finally, another professor invited me to join a small faculty group to share my research and writing agenda. This team met for thirty minutes prior to a required staff meeting to talk through their progress with publishing. They also openly voiced their frustrations. I found that I was not alone! Others were struggling through revisions, resubmissions, and rejections. They pointed out ways they had managed their barriers. As a support group, these colleagues understood the aggravations writers face as well as positive outcomes.

The value of collaboration and mentoring is often overlooked or condensed. Yet, many colleagues provided me with the assistance and direction that I needed – when I needed it most. Today I keep a running list of possible topics and look forward to writing again. But maybe more notable is the appreciation I feel toward my peers. One day soon, I hope to serve on the other side of this experience, helping another new faculty member who is just beginning the writing journey.

Mary Martin
Winthrop University

Five Strategies for Successful Co-Authoring of Articles

Collaborating is exhilarating, the comparison of research findings is intriguing, and working through the writing project with other authors is stimulating. The exchange of ideas will lead to better understanding of the topic. In addition, the comparison of research findings will produce even more ideas for further projects. This process can also be very challenging. Acceptance of friendly amendments helps to develop the cohesive relationship that joint writing demands. Generative writing, a term that Boice (1990) used when discussing the importance of writers gaining momentum and diminishing resistance, is one way authors create publishable articles. Writers should keep writing and researching their area of interest; they should never stop putting their ideas on paper. While each of us continues to write and publish individually, we have found the following strategies helpful in mastering successful collaborative writing.

Choosing a Topic

Topics should reflect the expertise and knowledge of the authors involved and include the audience as well as the publisher's needs. Topic selection requires the authors to decide on exactly what they want to explore. This process requires consensus by the authors. Agreeing on the topic will set the tone and lay the groundwork for the entire article. Make sure the topic is not too broad; instead, select a topic that you have a passion for and for which there is sufficient information to share. Decide on a topic that is relevant to current research inquiry, thus avoiding mundane repetition. Keep the topic in plain view and write toward this theme so you do not stray.

Outlines

The outline is the roadmap for getting from point A to point B. The outline lists goals, timelines, and deadlines. Once the outline has been compiled, authors decide on which sections they will each take as separate writing assignments. Henson, (2005) suggests that the writers use a flowchart to organize the article. Using flowcharts simplifies the writing assignment and presents steps to follow in chronological order with deadlines for completing each step. Deadlines are necessary in order to ensure that all authors involved are ready at the same time for editing, proofing, and commingling of the text. Concentrate on orderly steps in organizing your outline. This extra attention to detail will pay big dividends as you proceed with writing your article.

Develop a Writing Habit

Dedicate a set amount of time each day to the writing project. L. Belcher (2009), K.T. Henson (2005), and R. Boice (1990) have suggested that writing thirty minutes to two hours a day is sufficient. More than that amount of concentration on a writing project is stressful—marathons are not necessary in order to publish. Remember, there is no such thing as the perfect time to write. Whether you feel like it or not, you must develop a habit for writing. That is the only way to get the job done without major delays.

Revision and Rewriting

We revise an article a dozen times before sending it out. Make sure the article has correct conventional grammar, clear sentence structure, and sequential flow. Craft your article to be reader-friendly and make sure you use active not passive words. We have found that the ability to communicate well is the ability to use meaningful language that gives clarity to the particular audience you are attempting to reach. Good writing quality includes rhythm, symmetry, balance, cadence, and style, according to R. Dowis (1990). Oftentimes, while working on a writing project, you can become so engrossed in the construction of the article that the simplest mistakes are overlooked. It is helpful to have an outside set of eyes examine your completed writing project to check for small as well as large mistakes.

Structure Your Article According to the Submission Guidelines

Journals provide the writer with submission guidelines—follow them! The submission guidelines are important, and, if they are not followed, the article might be rejected automatically. Review the structure of the article to make sure that it fulfills all of the requirements of the guidelines. Checking for the correct style usage is an important aspect of complying with publication guidelines. Remember that the guidelines include both what the journal editors want to see, and what the editors do not want to see in your article (Adare 1995). Failure to comply with the submission guidelines will ultimately spell certain doom for the article.

References

Adare, S. (1995). What editors look for: How to write compelling queries, cover letters, synopses and book proposals, Thermopolis, WY, Cougar Imprints.

Belcher, W. (2009). *Writing your journal article in 12 weeks: A guide to academic publishing success*, Los Angeles, CA, Sage.

Boice, R. (1990). *Professors as writers: A self-help guide to productive writing*, Stillwater, OK, New Forums Press, Inc.

Henson, K.. (2005). *Writing for publication: Road to Academic advancement*, Boston, MA, Pearson.

Sherwood Thompson
William Phillips
Eastern Kentucky University

Virtual Collaboration

As administrators, especially those in Student Affairs, it is vital that we conduct scholarly activities as do our academic counterparts. Whether scholarship/research is something you truly enjoy or feel you "have to do," academic credibility goes a long way in building respectful partnerships in order to serve our students well.

One of the challenges we face in "writing for publication" (besides time) is finding another professional colleague with whom we want to collaborate on a project. Senior-level administrators (Cabinet level positions) are not always able to partner with colleagues from our own campuses. One means of collaboration is the use of professional networks and the creation of a collaborative project via the virtual world. Through these networks, one is able to ascertain the competency (at least perceived) level of colleagues, similar professional interests, and potential for partnership.

Benefits

Several benefits accrue from choosing virtual collaboration. This choice provides an opportunity for you to detach a project from your home institution by allowing you to work with others from a different type of institution with different experiences. If for some reason the project does not progress in the way it was intended, there is no impact on a day-to-day working relationship. Another benefit is that you are able to collaborate with others who possess similar interests and to test new theories or practices before bringing them to your home campus. In addition to your getting a different point of view, collaboration allows you to spread the workload on projects, thus creating a more efficient manner in completing multiple projects. Lastly, having another independent set of eyes serving as an editor on your work without the risk of alienation because of a personal relationship is helpful. The relationship is professional, not personal.

Challenges

Since others are counting on you to do your part, the project must be well organized and planned. Time cannot be wasted in doing the work of others (because it did not get done). Collaboration means carrying your share of the work. Meeting/working on the project in a virtual environment makes it difficult to do last-minute work by just stopping in and catching up with each other. The virtual meetings need to have purpose and specific agendas. A challenge in a virtual collaboration is trust since the day-to-day accountability is difficult to ensure because of the lack of daily contact. An agreement to be honest with each other on how the project is progressing from all involved is crucial. You need to be able to trust that everyone is doing his/her part and that no surprises will occur! One of the greatest challenges in a virtual collaboration project is "out of sight, out of mind." Very few day-to-day reminders (not seeing your partner) make it easy to put things off with the thought, "I will work on it later"—but later never comes. Trust comes into play as each partner holds the other accountable. Setting up an accountability process without being a "nudge" is difficult.

Steps

In order to maximize the benefits while minimizing the challenges in virtual collaboration, several steps can be instituted.

1. In order to reap the maximum benefits of the virtual partnership, making connections outside of your institution is crucial.
2. Before establishing any type of agreement on a project or even establishing a virtual collaborative relationship, prudently assess the strengths and limitations you bring to the project. "What can your partner expect and not expect from you"—remember honesty is the key! Also, narrow the list of interests that you would be willing to work on; as is the case with a dissertation topic, if it does not grab you, it is difficult to stay interested and to bring it to completion.
3. During your assessment, be willing to take the lead on a topic for collaboration. If something really interests you, do not let someone divert you to another topic. Choose the topic and then the partner, not the other way around. Even though you may respect the other person, working on a project that is of limited interest to you will create a challenge in getting it done at a high level of quality.
4. As with any project, the upfront planning is crucial. Put together a formal or even an informal proposal outlining the topic area; list your strengths and what you bring to the project, desired outcomes, your expectations of the partner(s), and tentative timeframe that will clearly define and communicate the project. Such a list is beneficial in recruiting a potential virtual collaborator, as well as a potential publisher.
5. Lastly, even though you have taken the lead and put together the proposal, a key to collaboration is the "give and take" of the relationship. Be willing to be flexible and

communicate what is negotiable or not negotiable when approaching potential partners. Keep in mind what is in the best interest of the project.

Summary

The thought of doing a project via the virtual world may be uncomfortable, but when done correctly and for the right reason, it can be a very positive experience. In addition to a job well done, you have expanded your professional network, established yourself as a professional in more venues, and fulfilled an essential part of being a scholar, adding to the body of knowledge for your profession. Good luck!

James Conneely
Eastern Kentucky University

An International Learning Community: Successful Vehicle for Scholarship

It is almost 10 years into the new millennium at which time, most education institutions declared that they were preparing teachers and students for the 21st century. In this era demanding education reform—higher student achievement—there has been much debate about programs and policies driving initiatives at the local, state, national, and international levels. Though there have been much conversation and corresponding new initiatives, schools and teachers around the world faces many of the same challenges: public accountability, evolving and ever-changing standards, increasingly stringent calls for higher performance with fewer resources, growing number of challenging students, shrinking teaching forces, calls for increased integration of technologies, and reform in educator preparation at all levels.

As our 21st world flattens, we in education must look outside our own sphere of comfort and develop research initiatives across the world; thus we seek international models and vehicles for international scholarship. Georgia Southern University College of Education faculty, beginning in 2001, have taken a national/international lead in developing an International Learning Community (ILC) and research agenda with colleagues in England, Wales, and China.

An International Learning Community is one example of a successful vehicle for scholarship. However, based on the experience of Georgia Southern University's ICL colleagues, it requires a comprehensive development and implementation plan that includes the following (see page 80):

Procedural Steps	'Words to the Wise'
Institution Selection ■ Comparable Institutions (size, mission, research interests) ■ Leaders with similar interests	ILCs based on personal contacts of individual members are likely to disappear with personnel changes.
Clearly Defined Mission ■ Develop and post (web page) goals, mission, purpose. ■ Develop an interdisciplinary and inter-institutional Advisory Board to oversee the work	ILCs must have a clearly defined mission, purpose, and goals. These will likely include activities other than research—student/faculty exchanges, shared conferences, etc.
University and College Commitment ■ Ensure an understanding of the importance of the work ■ Seek support at all levels for the work (leadership, faculty and students)	If you wait, you lose. Few, if any institutions, will have "upfront" funds to support all the work. In times of budget issues, few are looking for new 'funding opportunities' for their limited resources. Understanding and valuing the work increases the likelihood of financial and other support.
Partner with other programs/units on campus ■ Broaden the scope of the work to include others ■ Develop interdisciplinary working teams.	"Resource partnering" with other units enables the work: Example: Multi-task--supervise exchange students, study abroad, or conference attendance AND data gathering on same trip.
Scholarship Redefined Internationally ■ Develop interdisciplinary research interests on all campuses, then match across campuses ■ Communicate, communicate, communicate within and across institutions ■ Network with existing international organizations (associated with most disciplines) ■ Celebrate successes	Stay focused on the mission, goals of each partner institution. A single focus on individual interests can result in ILC failures with personnel changes. Communication within and across institutions and with discipline specific international organizations provides support for meetings, research discussions, presentation options, exhibits, etc. Shout scholarly successes from inter-disciplinary roof-tops.

Lucinda Chance
Georgia Southern University

The ABCs of Writing Groups at Small Universities

Finding time to write in academia is a problem that all professors have from time to time. This problem is more pronounced at institutions where professors teach 4 classes each term. This is an issue that professors and researchers at smaller schools and universities often discover soon after starting a new job at a school of this type. Given that many smaller institutions expect their faculty to publish and conduct research on par with their larger state institutions, it is imperative that faculty members at these smaller institutions develop relationships with their colleagues to aid in research, writing, and other creative areas of their work. To assist with this process, I suggest that faculty members at small institutions create writing groups to tap into the creative energies that fellow faculty members have to co-author articles, books, and research studies. Teachers of all levels are renowned for their cellular existence; that is, they stay within their own world and rarely collaborate with colleagues on joint projects. In what follows, I outline a plan for getting the most out of the collaborative writing/researching process.

A-Announce: In this stage, announce at a faculty meeting that you are organizing writing groups based on mutual interests. In this stage you may want to have faculty members send you an email with their relevant publications and/or their current writing and research interests. After you have compiled a list of your faculty and their writing interests, you can begin to form writing groups. This first stage is the most important because many of your faculty are simply unaware of the fact that their academic interests are the same (or similar) as others at your institution.

B- Break into groups: Once writing/research interests have been disseminated to the faculty in your college or division, faculty members can be organized around broad interests. At this stage, you simply want to get like-minded colleagues to have conversations about their interests. It is not necessary that everyone agree on a single, narrow topic, but rather that the conversation gets started towards collaboration and shared work towards publication of their ideas and work. This step in the process can be easily achieved at a faculty or in-service meeting.

C-Collaborate: In this stage, faculty members begin to narrow their interests from the broad ideas that brought them together in the previous stage. When group members collaborate, they are simply looking for narrow interests *within* the group. Group members need to begin to think towards pooling their resources. Groups can do this by asking the following questions: 1) Has anyone published in this area before? 2) Does anyone teach a class that is directly related to this topic? 3) Does anyone have a review of literature on this topic, and if so, how recent was it compiled? By asking these sorts of questions, you get a good sense of where the group "is" and what steps need to be taken next in the information gathering.

D-Decide: Once the resources and previous work completed for writing/research have been determined, group members should decide on a clearly defined, concise idea on which to write. This stage is particularly important because it allows for intense focus on a topic. In doing collaborative writing projects, writers have a tendency to go "off on their own tangent," writing or researching a topic that is uniquely their own. This "selfishness" can quickly derail a collaborative writing project. To avoid this issue, the group needs to decide on group roles or assign specific sections of a topic to each person in the group. For instance, one person could write the introduction, another could write a section on conceptual framework, another could write a literature review, and another could write the summary of findings. The combinations for division of labor are endless; the important part is to make sure that each person in the group has a distinct role to play in the eventual completion of the writing project. You can also have roles assigned to the team members that are not section specific, but role or job specific. For example, one person is responsible for making sure that all of the references and citations are in order, another person can check for grammar errors, and another can look for potential journals.

E-Evaluate: Once roles have been assigned and a first draft of the paper has been written, the group needs to evaluate their work. This area is perhaps the most sensitive area to navigate when working with others on collaborative projects. Many people are easily offended when you criticize their work. In this stage, you must make sure that you are constructive in your criticism of others' work, while keeping an eye (and the group's focus) on the end goal. As anyone who has ever attempted professional/scholarly writing knows, the writing process is just that—a process. In collaborative writing, there is definitely a "give-and-take" component that is an inherent part of the process. Go into this stage with a stance of compromise and collegiality.

F-Final Draft: After your manuscript has gone through several revisions and rewrites, it is now time to shape your work into a final draft. Your main goals in this step are to check your grammar and style and work to shape the narrative into a concise, clear statement of your group's work. Also, you may want to consider having several outside readers look at your work; many times our writing/research makes sense to us because we are "so close" to the project. Outside readers are great for overcoming this aspect of writing.

G-Goal: You have reached the final step in the group writing process! This is the step where you will send your work to a journal or other outlet for publication. If your work is not accepted the first place you send it, this is ok. Take the editor's comments into consideration, revise, and send to another journal. Again, this is another "process" aspect of writing for academia. Kenneth Henson's book *Writing for Publication: Road* *to Academic Advancement* (2005) is a must read for anyone who is new to the writing/publishing process. If you are beginning this process, this book is invaluable.

Prentice T. Chandler
Athens State University

A Writing and Publication Group Becomes an Intellectual Community

Have you ever been a part of a thriving intellectual community? Many scholars have experienced a sense of community while exploring ideas with graduate school colleagues or among small groups of university faculty. When describing ideal environments for doctoral students and faculty, Walker and his co-authors list several essential characteristics of a vibrant intellectual community: They have a shared purpose, they are diverse and multigenerational in membership, they are flexible and forgiving, and all participants are respectful and generous (Walker et. al, 2008, pp. 125-27).

We are writing to report on our experiences within a writing and publication group established to provide an environment of intellectual community. While all members have either completed doctorates, are currently working on doctoral degrees, or aspire to begin a doctoral program at some point in their careers, our setting is not within a doctoral program. We are a free-standing group called Student Affairs Administrators Doing Research (SAADR). Our intellectual community includes nine members who are staff, faculty members, or graduate students related to student affairs work at Baylor University.

Our common purpose is to learn about research and publication by sharing our work with group members who provide feedback. Accountability among the members of the group pushed us to see abstract ideas through to the publication stage in a timely manner and to increase our quality due to the feedback of careful readers. The concept of collegial peer review is not new for those accustomed to scholarship and research, but we hope this brief narrative of the formation and experiences of our group will serve as a practical guide for readers who wish to undertake a similar effort at their universities with an atmosphere of intellectual community.

Getting started: This group technique has been used in doctoral programs to encourage writers through the more isolated stages of dissertation preparation, and the organizer of our group drew on his experiences as a doctoral student. While writing his dissertation, he met regularly with his dissertation director and several other Ph.D. students to discuss their research. The organizer's invitation was simple: "Come to the table and see what happens." He personally invited student affairs staff members interested in writing and publication, and possibly doctoral studies, along with a few faculty and masters-level students.

We all came together for a 90-minute meeting twice each month. We met as equals, even though outside the group, some of us supervised others, and some of us taught and graded others in classes. Those hierarchies melted away in our meetings. Everyone's ideas were treated with respect, and criticism was both given and received well, though for some of us, learning to make ourselves vulnerable to criticism was part of the learning process. For example, one member sent out a piece for the group to read and critique. The accompanying email said, "Here it is; be nice!" This charge led to a great discussion in our next meeting about how critique is not always "nice" in the sense of being polite or gentle. The kindest thing we can do for one another is to be honest in our feedback, though a respectful tone is essential. We expressed how the writer's instructions to us could inhibit honest feedback. This discussion was fruitful for all of us, but most particularly for the writer, who explored honestly his feelings of insecurity when submitting written work. Examples such as this one demonstrate that the group was much more than a task-focused writing group; there is a social and emotional component within our intellectual community that enhances our experience.

Group structure. Over the three years of its existence, the size of the group fluctuated as members moved to other institutions, entered doctoral programs, or graduated. In our opinion, the optimum size for such a group is approximately six to ten people; our typical pattern has been four administrators/staff, three faculty members, and two graduate students. Our organizer established it as a closed group, meaning that membership was by invitation only and the group's boundaries were solid, rather than permeable. Member selection could sometimes be a difficult process simply because it was always collaborative and unanimous. When a group member departed, the remaining individuals brought forward the names of other colleagues who displayed an aptitude for or interest in research and publication. Of those names, one or two were chosen unanimously for invitation to the group. If none were agreed upon unanimously, the group members continued to suggest more names. While this invitation-only, closed-group model may sound off-putting or even pretentious, it contributes greatly to the effectiveness of the group. Faculty, administrators, and students rarely find themselves in a situation where everyone is on equal footing and no one holds authority over the others. Some graduate students, for example, do not feel comfortable addressing a professor by first name, even though this standard was an important requirement within our group and set a tone for the type of interactions that took place during meetings.

Trust is an essential component of the group dynamic. It is therefore important that group members spend time building deep, sustainable relationships with one another rather than orienting a new set of members each meeting. Once you find the right mix of people, we recommend you stick with it for at least one year before making changes. Sometimes it seems hard to exclude people simply because they do not seem to "fit" with the group, but you always have the opportunity to encourage them to establish another one. The more research groups the better!

Expectations and meetings. When an individual joined our research group, we told him/her that we operated under one primary expectation: that everyone showed up. Attendance and participation were by far the most important factors in the group's success. We had some secondary expectations that included bringing forward research ideas, offering innovation, giving constructive criticism, and providing edits in a timely manner, to name a few. Even if people attended a meeting with no ideas of their own, they could offer valuable advice and criticism to the rest of us.

Our meetings always began with a personal exchange as we updated one another on our lives, jobs, and studies. This format allowed us to form relationships on a deeper level and provided insight into how individuals' research or knowledge interests developed throughout their lives. The meeting continued as we began the work of sharing, reviewing, and conceptualizing. Below are listed multiple examples of meeting activities and discussion topics:

1. Review of an article-in-progress
2. Collaborative speculation on which journal or publication might be likely to accept a group member's written work
3. Discussion of applications to doctoral programs
4. Proposing a collaborative project among members with common interests
5. Editing of surveys for a group member's empirical research project
6. Celebration of publication.

After the first year, our organizer left the university, so each year since, one group member has volunteered to serve as the facilitator. He or she is responsible for scheduling meetings, sending out reminders, and writing and printing the agenda. In our research group, everyone's name appeared on the agenda at each meeting along with a list of current projects. We tried not to end a meeting without at least touching base with each person at the table about his or her projects. If someone was operating under a strict deadline, then we gave him/her the first opportunity to speak up. The primary thing to remember here is that as long as the group members continue to dialogue about how things are working and what routines need to be changed, meetings will continue to be productive.

Outcomes. In addition to co-authoring a publication with two faculty members during my year in the cohort, I (Emily, a graduate student) was able to forge and maintain relationships with faculty and staff from across the university whom I might not have met otherwise. Their knowledge and experiences helped me greatly as I completed my degree and thought more particularly about my future. I also became aware of many research areas and journals that were completely new to me.

I (Laine, a faculty member) found great excitement in the innovation and energy of younger members as well as the accountability for me to meet with the group and make progress on my publications. I also loved being able to give feedback to a paper or project, without the usual accompanying grade. It was very freeing for me as a teacher to help students improve their writing with formative feedback, without having to give a summative letter grade.

One of the most obvious benefits of this group is the opportunity to become a published author. We didn't measure individual success by number of publications, but we valued one another's work and wanted it to be disseminated as much as possible. This small publication is a good demonstration of our group at work; we found our way to collaboration on this piece, but we would not have explored this interest together without our group. As usual, our group read this article and provided feedback to us!

While research and publication may seem a daunting task to full-time faculty, administrators, and students who undertake it on their own time, joining a research group such as this one can aid in reaching your goals and provide much-needed accountability and camaraderie. We encourage you to gather a group of people who have publication goals and begin nurturing your own intellectual community!

Reference

Walker, George E., Golde, Chris M., Jones, Laura, Conklin Bueschel, Andrea, & Hutchings, Pat (2008). *The Formation of Scholars: Rethinking doctoral education for the twenty-first century.* San Francisco: Jossey-Bass.

T. Laine Scales
Emily Rodgers
Baylor University

Stalking the Reluctant Professor: How to Find a Mentor without Getting Arrested

Finding a good mentor to guide you in researching and publishing is often a daunting and seemingly impossible task. Questions that often nag us include: Whom should I approach? How do I prepare? Am I being appropriately assertive or stalking? As students, we often think that faculty members are gods among men (or goddess among women) who are infallible and unapproachable. Of course, deep down we know this is false, but hierarchy in academia persists and is as real as our fears. If only we had a clear list of rules for academic success. This article was written to fulfill that need… at least with regard to how to find a good mentor without having to resort to breaking the law.

The first key to finding a research adviser is preparation. Think about what interests you and have some ideas of what you would like to research. Once you have an idea, actually start doing a literature review. One of the first questions that a potential advisor will ask you is whether a particular project has already been done. If you are able to show a professor that you have already done some background research and that what you are interested in is undiscovered territory, you will be a much more attractive candidate than someone who is less prepared.

The next step, after preparation, is doing your research on the faculty. The key to choosing the correct mentor is picking someone whose interests align with yours. Thus you will not necessarily be paired up with that sociable and comedic professor who is everyone's favorite. If he is not interested in the same things that interest you, then he will not be as interested in *you*. The advisor who is invested in you will be much more likely to lead you to a publication than one who is unmotivated by your research topic. Also, the best mentors provide one-on-one guidance, so consider someone who has fewer obligations and mentees. Finally, sometimes no members of the faculty at your institution are interested in your research interests. In this situation, one option that many students fail to consider is finding a mentor outside of their institution. Also, if you are unable to find your "perfect mentor," then consider changing your interests to match the mentor's. If publishing is high on your list of things to accomplish, then swallow your pride and find something else that intrigues you within the realm of your potential mentor's interests.

Now that you have successfully prepared for battle and picked your champion, the next step is to actually approach the mentor. However, before you approach that person, make sure that you consider the timing. Do not approach a potential advisor when she is in the process of applying for a research grant or when he is planning his wedding. Advisors are much more likely to accept another project when they are not busy. Some good times that one should consider approaching a mentor include at the end of a semester or right before a long break when they have probably wrapped up most of their other tasks. Consider making an appointment rather than just dropping by their office. This shows that you respect their time and understand they are busy.

When approaching a potential advisor for help, remember that you are not a student, you are a salesperson. Sell yourself. Faculty members are humans just like the rest of us and as such they often want to know what is in it for them. How do you accomplish this? First, explain to them in detail how your interests align with theirs. Make sure that you express your interest in what they have accomplished so far and how your project will add valuable information to the field. The key to getting an advisor's attention is making explicit how your research answers the "so what?" question. If you believe that your idea matters and will make a significant contribution to the field, explain this with conviction. Also, remember the literature review that you did? Bring in articles to show the potential mentor how prepared you are and that you have a strong work ethic. Come in with set timeline, measurable goals, and ways to keep yourself on track, including deadlines for your literature review and ethics proposal. This detailed plan communicates that you are a self-starter who is motivated to learn and does not need babysitting. It also communicates to a mentor what s/he stands to benefit: a quick co-publication, a service commitment to the university fulfilled, a research protégé created.

Finally, remember that you are always being observed by the faculty in your program. If you behave as an unreliable student in classes, then it will be very difficult to convince faculty that you will be a reliable researcher and mentee. Make sure that you show your potential mentors through your daily interactions that you are a student who loves learning, works hard, meets deadlines, does quality work, and handles criticism well. Your attitude matters: genuine kindness and a lack of entitlement are vital. Be responsible in your day to day interactions, and you will set yourself up for success.

Kadie Fritz
Danielle Stevens-Watkins
Elise Shaffer
Robert Mattson
Sara Zachary
Jessica Rickart
Dede Wolfarth
Spalding University

Why Is It So Darn Hard To Get That Article Pushed Out The Door?

For professors to be excellent educators, they must continue to learn and grow. This concept has become increasingly true since technological advances have caused an explosion of discoverable information in recent years. As online educational options continue to expand, university scholars will be challenged to compete for market share, a challenge that will require scholars to redouble their efforts to take command of all of the trustworthy knowledge in their respective fields. Such scholarly endeavors include the process of doing research and the dissemination of pedagogical frameworks as well as publishing research findings in scholarly journals and/or presenting at conferences. Professors must strive to remain experts in their fields or risk irrelevancy and extinction.

Although faculties at most teaching institutions are evaluated on the three areas of teaching, service, *and scholarship*, realities tend to reduce scholarship to the lowest priority. While the time requirements of effective teaching constantly demand the professor's attention, and a steady stream of committee work and service requirements are advanced by one's institution, scholarship is something that the professor usually has to initiate on his or her own.

Professors meet the teaching requirements because there is a schedule for when the classes meet, regular inquiries from students, and deadlines implicit in class preparation and the return of graded assignments. Likewise, service opportunities often involve other people's schedules (e.g., a committee meeting) taking place at a particular time with a particular task and deadline. Scholarship, however, does not usually come with such external motivators. Therefore, even with the best of intentions, professors too often postpone scholarly writing until later. Until next week. Until next summer. Until . . .

Further, even if the professor is disciplined enough to carve out that three-hour Friday afternoon writing period and to actually stick with it past the second Friday of the semester, writing is frequently a solitary pursuit. Faculty often receive immediate emotional support from their colleagues and students in the pursuit of teaching and service, but it is typically denied them in most scholarly pursuits, at least until that work is finished (a presentation is given or an article is published). Just as going to the dentist's office is often postponed for a more pleasant activity, time spent on scholarship too often gives way to more emotionally-supported duties.

In an effort to mitigate those circumstances, a group of pre-tenured faculty at Eastern Kentucky University decided to create a scholarly publishing support group. Using a play on the phrase *publish or perish*, the group named their endeavor *Publish and Relish* (buh-dum-dum) and decided that not only would the "food brings fellowship" mantra be employed, but that participants would be encouraged to *relish in* their success when publications came to fruition.

Every three weeks, participants gather to hear short presentations given by the participants on topics that are currently "under construction." From time to time, topics related to the research and scholarly writing process (e.g., the IRB approval process, using parametric statistical procedures such as ANOVAs or t-tests, utilizing qualitative research procedures) are chosen by the participants to refresh or enhance their knowledge.

Participating faculty agreed to:
1) create a network of "critical friends" who would support one another in the research and writing processes and chart the progress of group members;
2) discuss questions and common concerns participants may have concerning research and getting articles published—all in a friendly, supportive atmosphere;
3) commit to deadlines for which the other members would hold the researcher/writer accountable;
4) help find editors for one another's writings within or outside of the group; and
5) provide a place for participants to celebrate submission and publication success.

In these ways, participants are consistently encouraged to keep research on their radar screens year round. This rather simple cooperative group accountability contributes to an on-going focus. "What gets inspected gets respected."

At every meeting, each participant shares 2-3 short-term goals that he/she wants to accomplish within the next three weeks. A goal can be as simple as finding a journal suitable for a project one is working on and learning its publication requirements. Or, turning that "rough" rough draft into something readable. Or, doing final edits on an article and submitting it.

A simple list is compiled at the meeting, and the list is e-mailed to the group at the end of the meeting. That way, each group member knows what he/she committed to, and the other group members are reminded of what the others are working on. At the next meeting, the group members report their success in accomplishing the goals. While the deadlines are self-imposed, and the only consequences are simply some good-natured teasing about *not having your homework* (and the passing out of Milk "Duds"), the mere existence of the deadlines puts scholarship on a more equal footing with the areas of teaching and service.

J. Jeannette Lovern
Richard Day
Eastern Kentucky University

Collaboration Is King: Five Tips For Publishing Research Papers

Most scholars collaborate with their colleagues at some point in their career. The challenge is thinking beyond the confines of academe. That's what we did, and our reward was not one, but two scholarly publications. In our research papers, we shared our method and results from a multi-year research project we undertook to collaborate with public relations professionals to develop and validate a rubric tying students' success in the academic world to their career readiness. We focused on (1) ensuring the academic concepts and dimensions within the rubric were the learning skills students in public relations studies need; and (2) ensuring those dimensions are professionally anchored.

In our case, the rubric was for a multi-section public relations writing course, and our collaborators were faculty who teach the course and also public relations professionals in Chicago. Because research is notably sparse on the collaborative process involving professionals and academics, this collaboration was our key to unlocking the door to editor interest.

Through our literature search, we found few academic researchers had brought together the faculty who actually teach and evaluate a student's work and professionals whose ultimate test of the student's knowledge and skills is a job offer. With further research, we identified the Delphi method as a useful means of collecting and distilling knowledge and reaching consensus among group members.

Tip One: Do something different. Academic literature is full of extensions of tried-and-true approaches to research. Think more broadly about the benefits to accrue from your research. Relevancy is important, so ground the process in real-world applications.

We started our research by using the Delphi method with a group of seven highly-regarded, senior-level public relations professionals. We identified skills, knowledge and abilities (SKA) that professionals expect of entry-level graduates. Simultaneously, we applied the Delphi method to arrive at consensus on these same SKAs among eleven faculty who teach the PR writing course. Then, we compared the results and used our findings to refine the final version of the rubric.

Tip Two: Develop a system. We utilized the continuous improvement system to drive us toward more informed results, which create a richer research experience. The system kept us on track, and enabled us to gather smaller, more focused data sets. Ergo, richer experience equals a deeper pool of results for analysis. Targeted analysis means a more interesting paper more likely to grab the reviewer's interest.

The more we learned, the more we wanted to write. Initially, we wanted to tell all we knew to anyone who would read our findings. Eventually, we realized we needed discipline to avoid diluting the authority of the research. So, we decided to address the work in two separate papers. We published our first research paper as an eight-step process for academics (Allen & Knight, 2009). Then, adding another collaborator to the mix, we published a second paper on the validation of that rubric (Knight, Tracy & Allen, 2010). Each was a better paper for its enforced brevity.

Tip Three: Focus. Determine your key message. This task was the most challenging for us. We asked ourselves "what" – that is, what about the topic would interest the targeted reader? Then we trimmed our writing to address how we got our results. We went beyond the basics and answered the Five Golden Questions: Why? Because? Says who? So what? Why should the reader care? Remember, to distinguish your work from the body of literature the message must be able to be grasped in the five seconds a reader spends scanning your paper.

As our papers became more focused, we found there were nuggets of information appropriate for expanded groups of readers. By using a new lens to view our work, we were able to adapt our research and the results to interest broader audiences.

Tip Four: Examine your scholarship and research from myriad angles. Academics naturally approach academic publications as repositories for their scholarship and research. However, we linked our academic discipline with publications of professional organizations. We found these professional publications often trumpet what's new in the field. Just as collaborating with professionals may be novel to your scholarship, it also may be fresh to the industry. To gather insight, read professional journals to learn what the reviewers look for in a publishable paper. Very often, the style of writing is endemic to that profession or industry. Tailor your writing, and don't hesitate to submit to those publications that appear appropriate for your work.

Finally, write like you speak, but write well. Wading through academic-speak is deadly. Who among us says, "A considerable amount of research was done"; or, "Results will be presented"? We are more likely to say, "Our research took two years," or "We will present. . . ." Clear, concise, and compelling writing means holding ourselves accountable for telling it straight. It means resisting the urge to hide behind lofty-sounding but empty words and phrases.

Tip Five: Be respectful of the editorial policies and the publication's standards for well written papers. Each of our papers required revisions, and the reviewer's comments provided useful guidance. When the reviewers send their comments, revise your work. In your resubmission, explain the changes, why you made them, and how they make the paper stronger. If you've ever been a reviewer, you know this explanation makes their job easier.

We know research and writing is not for the faint of heart. We discovered there are no failsafe approaches for the publishing scholar, but we learned, with thought, time, energy and effort, there are successes to be had.

John E. Knight
University of Tennessee at Martin
Sandra Allen
Columbia College Chicago

Using Authentic Data In Classroom Exercises

As a culminating assignment the students in our School Finance course are required to gather all the budget data from a school district and create a presentation to the class as if we were the community voters in that district. These presentations must include the authentic data from the school district both current and past and propose the increase/decrease in the tax rate to the homeowners as well as reflect the official CPI (Consumer Price Index). Rather than fictitious data sets and case studies, we use the realities that the different schools represent in our class and discuss the nuances of these presentations.

Rural, suburban, and urban districts are almost always represented in our varied student body and thus the presentations present a very real picture of what school finance implications look like in our immediate and regional area. Students usually team up for these presentations since we often have two students from the same school district in class. They may also choose to use the district they live in rather than the one they work in. This in-class exercise has proven beneficial in the past, and we always check to see how close we are to the reality of passing that school budget in the community as our class typically ends just prior to the budget voting date in our state.

New York has a common budget voting date for all communities across the state. At times the naiveté of the students coupled with their positive research strategies can uncover interesting elements and lead to conclusions that may differ from the local district, creating great topics of conversation as well as preparing our students for the realities of data-driven research.

Greg K. Gibbs
St. Bonaventure University

A Scholarly Assignment

I want my students to appreciate the value of both research and ethical application. It is my belief that to be ethical leaders my students need to be knowledgeable professional educators who truly embrace the importance of success for all students. And, being knowledgeable educators means keeping abreast of current publications, knowing how to gather and interpret data, and, ultimately, publishing their findings and recommendations.

Too often as instructors we *talk* about student engagement and then proceed with making our own assignments based on what we think is best. To truly *walk the talk*, it behooves us to encourage our students to become active participants in their learning. An assignment that works for me is to have my students review their School Improvement Plans. On a basic level, completion of this assignment is a mini scholarly writing. Students are asked to identify an area for improvement based on the gathering and interpreting of the data. The ultimate goal is for my students to recommend appropriate program changes for implementation. Through this assignment, students can develop connections between their experiences and current research. Simply put, it means that students will need to think, and I feel that the value of leadership as educators is based on the value of thinking. And, to be skilled in thinking, we need to be skilled in asking the difficult questions.

Activity:

Assume you are the principal of your school. Review your School Improvement Plan and identify one goal in the area of curriculum improvement that you would like to see achieved in your school within the next three years. Why did you select this goal (use data to support your goal), how will you assess, how will you use these results for program changes? What do you want to see as results? How does this benefit all children?

1. Define
   a. Goal
      Rationale for selection
      Data
   b. Activities
   c. Learner needs and characteristics
   d. Budget schedule (If appropriate)
2. Design
   a. Strategy for implementation
   b. Predicted outcomes
   c. Assessment

3. Results
   a. Effectiveness of goal
      Met the needs of the varied needs and interests of your learners
   b. Areas of weakness
     Tests
     Projects

Patricia Hoehner
University of Nebraska at Kearney

Co-Creating with Students: Establishing Trust in a Student-Factulty Research Group

Trust can facilitate learning, productivity, and motivation in a variety of academic settings. One setting in which trust is vital is a student-faculty research group, also known as a Research Interest Group (RIG). A RIG is a small group of students and professors who are interested in a similar research topic and collaborate to pursue an in-depth exploration of this topic. By joining a RIG, a student has the opportunity to establish connections with both other students and the professor who leads the group. These connections are imperative for mentorship from the professor as well as friendships with peers. This social support is critical for success in arduous undergraduate and graduate programs. Additionally, students in a doctoral level program may find a dissertation topic through connections established within the RIG. Therefore, these groups enable students to find a creative outlet within an academic setting and establish connections for future projects.

Some general guidelines for establishing trust in a RIG may be helpful. Overall, establishing normalcy within a RIG seems to be an effective way to promote trust. Guidelines for establishing normalcy include meeting regularly, finding committed members, closing the group to new members after a specified period of time, and keeping the meetings informal. An optimal number of students is approximately four to eight members. Also, when an idea for publication credit is first brought into the RIG, authorship order is agreed upon in advance so group members know who is taking the lead in terms of workload. Establishing authorship order from the beginning decreases problematic frustrations and setbacks later on. The first author should be responsible for the most work for that particular publication. Rotating first authorship can also ensure that everyone in the group gets an equal opportunity to be the first author.

Establishing trust between students in a RIG can also increase the group's productivity. To establish trust among students, the students should feel comfortable bringing new ideas into the group without fear of rejection by others. Additionally, the students must hold each other accountable for completing the work assigned to them. Individuals who trust others have been found to contribute more in social situations when they are held accountable (De Cremer, Snyder, & DeWitte, 2001). Therefore, accountability enables the group to be more productive, and productivity is essential for successful publication efforts. One tangible example of this accountability is the act of establishing, and following, agreed upon deadlines for assignments. Another practical example is breaking a large project into smaller goals so that feedback is ongoing, timely, and more likely to be positive.

Additionally, the professor must trust the students within a RIG. If the professor does not trust the students, s/he may be more likely to set up a controlling climate. Professors who operate in these types of climates may be more likely to be critical and show more disapproval towards their students (Leroy, Bressoux, Sarrazin, & Trouilloud, 2007). Therefore, controlling climates decrease student motivation and thus hinder productivity. Additionally, if a professor lacks trust for his or her students, the students may become distrustful of the professor. A venomous environment directly impacts a group's ability to reach its goals.

Another aspect of trust that is necessary within a RIG is the trust of the professor by the students. The professor should be approachable, supportive, and open to new ideas that the students bring into the group. Another way to promote trust is to allow time for student-driven agenda items (e.g., how to write a vita; how to find a good practicum site) as well as research-driven topics. When professors support their students' motivational needs, including informative feedback, personal progress, and task mastery, professors contribute to the internalization of autonomous motivation in their students (Leroy et al., 2007). Autonomous motivation refers to the quality of self-motivation, which leads directly to group productivity. Additionally, the professor should understand that students are busy with multiple obligations, and should set realistic work parameters and expectations. It may be helpful to set deadlines much earlier than the publisher's deadlines so that they may be pushed back if the students become engulfed with other obligations. This flexibility ensures that approaching deadlines will not overwhelm the students.

Joining a RIG can be an effective way to support successful student-faculty research projects. However, trust is an essential aspect of learning, productivity, and motivation within a RIG, all of which are necessary for reaching group goals. To promote trust within a RIG, students must learn to trust each other and their professor just as the professor must learn to trust the students.

References

De Cremer, D., Snyder, M., & DeWitte, S. (2001). The less I trust, the less I contribute (or not)? The effects of trust, accountability and self-monitoring in social dilemmas. *European Journal of Social Psychology, 31,* 93–107.

Leroy, N., Bressoux, P., Sarrazin, P., & Trouilloud, D. (2007). Impact of teachers' implicit theories and perceived pressures on the establishment of an autonomy supportive climate. *European Journal of Psychology of Education, 22,* 529-545.

Sara Zachary
Jessica Rickard
Elise Shaffer
Kadie Fritz
Robert Mattson
Dede Wolfarth
Spalding University

Getting Published as a Graduate Student

When I (Emily) first entered my masters program, I assumed that publication was something that graduate students only dreamt of, but never attained. It seemed a daunting task to use my precious spare time to write an article and undergo the rigors of submission, not to mention the fact that the submission-review-acceptance method was entirely unknown to me. Fortunately, I worked with several faculty and staff members who were able to demystify the whole process of publication for me, and by the time I graduated, I could list several scholarly articles and conference presentations on my résumé.

I (Laine) work with graduate students in my roles as Associate Dean in Baylor's Graduate School and Professor of Higher Education. An important part of my work is to identify graduate students who have the potential to be published, to help them develop their writing skills, and to find them publication outlets. Sometimes I accomplish this goal by inviting them into a piece I am working on, or sometimes I serve as coach and editor for their own work in order to facilitate and guide them through their first publication. We have outlined a few simple steps that graduate students can take to enter the enigmatic world of publication. These ideas are not exhaustive, but we have learned from experience that creativity and the willingness to make an extra effort can take you a long way.

Don't despise the day of small beginnings. Be willing to start with a minor project just to get experience and learn the process. You can't necessarily expect to be published in a top-ranked journal on your first try. Be willing to do some research to find a publication outlet that is more accessible, with a high acceptance rate. You might also consider the following options:
- Book reviews
- Encyclopedia entries
- Magazines of professional organizations
- Newsletters

Learn the ropes; everyone needs a proofreader. If a faculty member is working on a particularly lengthy or tiresome project, you might help him/her by proof-reading or editing. Sometimes this approach can lead to your contributing a small amount of original writing, which, depending on the professor, might lead to being listed as a co-author, or at least being mentioned in a footnote. This approach can be a great way to get involved in a publication, learn the ropes, and it doesn't require you to come up with an article topic or find a publisher.

Collaboration is key. The first thing I (Emily) learned about publication was revealed to me through the process of co-authoring with a more established scholar. Sometimes you might have the luxury of being approached by a faculty member and asked to write with him or her, but more often than not you have to think about how you might contribute to a professor's research and scholarship and then take the initiative to start a discussion. Regardless of how the relationship is established, there is much you can learn by working with a published scholar. Ask to be included on emails between the faculty member and the editorial staff of the publication to which you are submitting, when appropriate, so that you can keep track of each stage of submission and editing and learn how to handle the process from start to finish.

Be bold, but be respectful. You should always take some time to look into a professor's research interests and past scholarship before you plan to approach someone about co-authorship. By displaying familiarity with the body of work, you can better determine the ways in which you can be of help to one another. Faculty members are often in search of new and fresh ideas, so don't be afraid to show that you have them! Just be sure to build upon their past work as well.

Convert a conference presentation into an article. When you are given the opportunity to present at a conference, take it! Sometimes the best publications are born out of conference sessions that are well-received. Collecting feedback from presentation attendees can help guide you as you convert the presentation into a written document. Additionally, if you have co-presenters, they will most likely be willing to shoulder some of the authorship responsibility.

If at first you do succeed, try, try again. If you publish with a particular journal (even as the second or third author) and the editor is pleased with your work, he/she will be more likely to accept another piece from you in the future. Keep track of the contact information for the publications in which you appear because you never know when it might come in handy!

In summary, getting started with publication during your graduate school years will help you become familiar with the process early, and you will be well on your way in your first professional job or faculty role. This article is an example of how the two of us, professor and graduate student, worked together. Students bring fresh ideas, energy, and enthusiasm, while professors may use their experience to guide the process and connect to publication outlets. Just give it a try and you may be surprised how fulfilling it can be to share your ideas in print!

Emily Rodgers
T. Laine Scales
Baylor University

Check the Checker

Using electronic medical records with students can be an overwhelming task especially when it comes to checking the student's work at the end of the day. Pairing students to check each other's documentation not only saves on faculty time but increases the student's level of understanding with the electronic medical record. The faculty member is looking at screens of data that the students enter for the day, and this can be a mundane task but is one of vital importance. The student is looking at this data with open eyes and scrutinizes the data for incorrect or omitted data. Checking the checker is a system that increases student learning, assists the student in participating in peer evaluation, and assists with decreasing faculty workload. In terms of scholarship, the process points out to students the importance of getting information correct along with fostering in them a spirit of collaboration.

Nancy Kern-Manwaring
Miami University

New Directions

The other day we were lamenting how hard we had it in graduate school as would-be scholars: we could never find sufficient source material, the one copy machine in the library was always broken, the key text was always "missing" (or had been razored out of a journal), inter-library loan took weeks, and the typed copy of the manuscript had to be perfect. By comparison, today's scholars have too much source material: computers come with printers; the internet is the new inter-library loan and it's instant; and computers format the research, check it for mechanical errors, and allow for multiple drafts.

The point isn't that today's scholars have it easier, but that the scholarly world is ever evolving. Who back then pulling a dusty tome from the stacks ever thought of publishing in electronic journals? New tools for research appear as frequently as apps for our iPhone. While certainly not exhaustible, the following section points to a few of these opportunities and ways to exploit them (in a good way, of course).

New Directions in Scholarship

The defining moment in university-produced scholarship came in 1990 when The Carnegie Foundation for the Advancement of Teaching published *Scholarship Reconsidered* (San Francisco: Jossey-Bass). In the volume, its president, Ernest Boyer, concluded "that the work of the professorate might be thought of as having four separate, yet overlapping functions:

- The scholarship of discovery
- The scholarship of integration
- The scholarship of application
- The scholarship of teaching" (16+).

Over the past twenty years scholarship, though, has metamorphosized. As we've already mentioned, for instance, the scholarship of teaching was poorly defined, and so a distinction was made between scholarly teaching and the scholarship of teaching. Later, with the ascendancy of active learning and assessment's emphasis on student learning outcomes, the scholarship of teaching was repositioned as the scholarship of teaching and learning.

Early in our careers, and long before Boyer's work, we saw the need for a fifth category. We began publishing fiction, both of a serious and a popular nature, and at the same time a major growth in the field of English was in creative writing. Initially, for instance, Charlie was rejected for promotion because his publications were predominantly fiction. The field grew so quickly, and partly because it lacked its own scholarship, it was slow to be recognized. Gradually scholars began to produce work on creative writing, and the field gained acceptance; in fact, it became the major growth portion of the English major at the end of the last century.

This so-called scholarship of creativity (our university calls it "the scholarship of creative endeavors") still had a problem, at least in our eyes. Anyone who has ever written a short story or poem, created a piece of art, or written music understands that creativity doesn't make something out of nothing at all. David Kord Murray defines creativity as often *Borrowing Brilliance*. In other words, the creative artist must perform research. Shakespeare had to study Holinshed's *Chronicles* to write some of his plays, Nathaniel Hawthorne needed Caleb Snow's *History of Boston* to support *The Scarlet Letter*, and in order to become Brett Halliday's ghost for the *Mike Shayne Mystery Magazine* novellas we wrote, we had to know forty years of Shayne's fictional biography.

Yes, people who study brainstorming and the importance of perception shift and production blocking are forging a new area—though some would argue it's really still the scholarship of discovery—but creative artists are also practicing the scholarship of creativity. Admittedly, an oil painting, an aria, or a sonnet may utilize a non-traditional format for that scholarship, but some of the same kind of research used by the traditional scholar was employed to create the artifact. Don't creative works contribute to what Boyer calls "the stock of human knowledge, but also to the intellectual climate of a college or university" (17)? Therefore, faculty artists need to achieve recognition for their scholarship too.

Just as scholars have subsequently made a distinction between scholarly teaching and the scholarship of teaching and learning, so a related distinction is being made in another Boyer category, the scholarship of application. Back in 1990 Boyer noted that "Colleges and universities have recently rejected service as serious scholarship, partially because its meaning is so vague and often disconnected from serious intellectual work" (22). On the other hand, if a professor is engaged in some important service, applies his/her scholarly background to it, and then writes up perhaps a solution to a service problem, shouldn't there be such a thing as the scholarship of service? At Eastern, our new strategic plan defines one of our three major directions as regional stewardship, a movement encouraged and funded by our commonwealth's Council on Postsecondary Education (CPE). If an education professor adapts the traditional agricultural extension agency approach and creates education extension agents, writes up the plan, and shows the results, shouldn't this scholarship of service be acceptable? Maybe what the professor has accomplished is a new variation on Boyer's scholarship of integration by "making connections across the disciplines" (18). In fact, some have called this new direction the scholarship of engagement.

Closely related to this advance is what a colleague of ours, Judy Spain, has accomplished with another variation in the scholarship of service. As a business professor, she was asked annually to chair a committee to stage relevant theme weeks for business students, such as bringing in speakers and holding workshops on business ethics. What she decided to do was simply survey the faculty and students involved with pre- and post-testing. As a result, she was able to document attitudinal shifts, write up the research, and publish it. At some time all of us must perform the dreaded drudge of committee work on a departmental, college, or university level. Judy's solution to making lemonade out of lemons is what she now calls the scholarship of committee work. From a wider view, we would suggest that the typical tripartite division of a faculty member's job into teaching, scholarship, and service is more of a matrix wherein each component can be seen as part of the others, not as wholly separate entities.

Still another area of expansion is what the electronic revolution now affords us and will continue to do. The whole definition of publication continues to expand. No, we don't think that a professor who posts her newest poems on her office door has "published" them, but what about a colleague of ours in education who writes a daily blog on his website about his interactions with faculty, students, and issues in education? Admittedly, some of Richard's blogs veer closer to traditional scholarship by seeing an everyday event within some educational research perspective, while others don't pass that kind of stringent litmus test. We have another colleague who just created a wiki to help participants at our recent state conference on higher education explore its theme of creativity by commenting on various strategies for teaching creativity. The creation of the wiki itself fits within the traditional concept of discovery, and its process will subsequently use others to discover and refine current strategies of the pedagogy of creativity, thus falling within SOTL and the scholarship of creativity. Doesn't Rusty's wiki, then, qualify as scholarship (perhaps the scholarship of integration because it utilizes various Boyer categories)?

As scholars push the envelope, our traditional notions of scholarship will have to be re-tuned. Our basic core values of scholarship may stay the same, but outside-the-box scholars deserve credit for pushing the frontiers and going where no one has gone before. What interests us most is that these expansions piggy-back on extant scholarship, something scholars have been doing for centuries. At the same time a problem has reared its ugly head. Some universities, colleges, and departments have been slow to note the changes. University definitions of scholarship and promotion and tenure rubrics need to be annually rewritten to accommodate advancements in scholarship.

Perhaps the next great category of scholarship will be meta-scholarship—i.e., scholarship about scholarship ... wait a minute—isn't that sort of what this collection is doing?

Hal Blythe
Charlie Sweet
Eastern Kentucky University

Creating SOTL: An Experiment in Collaboration

Let's say that you have read this far and you have become convinced that you would like to try to collaborate on some research/scholarship, but you are not sure of a subject. What we would like to suggest is an experiment, a trial run if you will. If you're not interested, skip this section.

Collabowrite a SOTL note.

SOTL, as you will remember from a previous essay, is one of Boyer's four categories, the Scholarship of Teaching and Learning. It's also one of the newest types of scholarship and doesn't have a long tradition or body of work. On the other hand, as more university missions emphasize the centrality of teaching and learning, it is becoming a most important type.

Definition

While Boyer didn't do well with his explanation of SOTL in *Enhancing Scholarly Work on Teaching & Learning* (San Francisco: Jossey-Bass, 2006), Maryellen Weimer offers this simple definition: "published work on teaching and learning authored by college faculty in fields other than education" (19). Weimer also notes that SOTL falls between the poles of personal experience-based wisdom-of-practice scholarship and research scholarship that is usually isolated inquiry. Pat Hutchings and Lee Shulman in "The Scholarship of Teaching" (Change 31.5 [1999]: 13) offer four characteristics of SOTL:
- Being public
- Open to critique and evaluation
- In a form others can build on
- Involves question-asking inquiry and investigation, particularly around issues of student learning.

We would suggest an expanded list of characteristics:
- It is published/presented—i.e., it has appeared in the public arena.
- It invites criticism/others to join in the conversation.
- It is intentionally created to improve student learning; be it a tip, a tactic, a strategy, an approach, or a methodology, its central goal is student learning.
- It is more than teaching per se; in fact, it is often the specific application of more generalized theories about teaching.
- It is part of an organized investigation; at its basis, it has a problem solved, a practice analyzed, a question answered, or a theory investigated.
- It is framed differently by different fields and given differing degrees of credit by those fields.
- It is part of shared knowledge. It builds upon or exists within a web of other investigations.
- It may be innovative; it may have set out to do so deliberately or the practitioner may have stumbled onto a valuable insight.
- It reveals expertise whether in its content, methodology, or even the practitioner's experience.
- It notes sources, demonstrating a knowledge of proper documentation.
- It impacts student learning whether on a minor or major level.

In addition, you could find out a lot very quickly about SOTL by attending a conference devoted to that subject. Our state has an annual Conference on the Scholarship of Teaching and Learning in May, but the best are probably any of the Lilly Conferences on College Teaching and Learning. Hutchings, Bjork, and Babb have produced *The Scholarship of Teaching and Learning in Higher Education: An Annotated Bibliography*.

Getting Started

Now that you have some idea of what SOTL is, how do you get started? As usual, we have some suggestions:
- **Reflect upon your own teaching practices.** Don't begin with something major, huge, and abstract such as your teaching philosophy or something you might write upon your theoretical approaches for the Promotion & Tenure Committee. Instead, try for something smaller, more concrete, some practice you favor. For instance, do you like to start class with a daily quiz? Why? Do you think it is effective? Or do you have any policies you have added to your syllabus over the years? Why do you refuse to allow cellphones in your classroom?
- **Keep a journal.** Jot down some of these practices as well as some of your questions. You might even add your own comments to things that you experience directly or indirectly. For instance, while we're typing this essay, we just ran across a review of a

new Nicholas Carr book called *The Shallows* (2010) in which the reviewer reacts to the author's denial of laptop use in his classroom.

- **Cultivate some colleagues with whom you think you might like to collabowrite.** Maybe you have had to prepare a committee report together, or maybe someone has asked you to look at the beginning of an article s/he has written. Maybe you ran across an article the colleague recently published. Be active in your recruitment; the perfect person with the perfect article proposal is not going to email you or walk through your office door very often.
- **Select a colleague with whom to share these reflections and entries.** And listen to both of you. When we talk, we tend to emphasize the high points of what we have read. Sometimes it's the enthusiastic tone that keys us to an important piece of information, sometimes it's the new information we have added to the old, and sometimes what we hear is the echo of something we could develop. Maybe it's the irritation in your voice when you discuss that student who seems engrossed in Laptop Land, but not your class.
- **Shape this review into a (hypo)thesis.** Initially you might come up with something like "Laptops are interfering with student learning." As you talk it over, you might refine your idea to "Laptop owners are less likely to have deep learning experiences." Right now all you have is your own personal experience as the basis for your research. How valid is it?
- **Do some basic research.** You could Google key terms or use a number of data bases (e.g., EBSCOHOST). What we've found is that our best ideas follow the Stephen King Principle. The great horror writer came up with *Carrie* not just because at the school he was teaching in a teenage girl had her first visit from mother nature, but also because he was reading an article in *Life* magazine on telekinesis. The Stephen King Principle states that good ideas are often the confluence of two things; one of those things is often personal experience while the other is research that gives that experience a context. In other words, you might not become that irritated with The Laptop Kid if you hadn't just been glancing at a review of *The Shallows* in *The Wall Street Journal*. In basic research we've found two things you must do. One, when researching, start with the most recent publication and work backwards. Let the previous researchers do a lot of your work for you. Two, find the key/seminal articles around which all others seem to cluster.
- **Create an introduction.** Use the basic research to create a context for your investigation. Use some personal classroom experience that relates to this theoretic framework. These two steps can appear in either order. Finally, state your now-refined hypothesis.
- **Write a review of the literature section.** While your research took you throughout time like Dr. Who, take control of the space-time continuum and produce your results in chronological order.

- **Learn APA style.** We would have liked to bury this suggestion since for a lot of researchers, especially those trained in the arts (and MLA) mastering a format so foreign is difficult. You could collaborate with someone who knows the style. On the other hand, we tried doing so and received bad advice on the form. If the form is new to you, you will begin to notice how important the date of a piece of research is, something essential in both hard and soft sciences.
- **Set up some experiment/research project to test your hypothesis.** In educational research we have found three forms predominate. First, the holy grail of educational experiments seems to be pre- and post-testing of participants, usually students (but sometimes faculty and administrators). For instance, when we wanted to prove that our students were learning something in an American Literature class, we gave them a test the first day and the same basic test the last day; lo and behold, sixteen weeks had produced some student learning (at least on the bottom of Bloom's Taxonomy). Second, educational researchers love to change just one variable and then compare the results. For instance, if you were teaching two sections of the same class, you might give the same test to two groups: one that was allowed to use cellphones and laptops during class and one that wasn't. Third, educational researchers love satisfaction surveys. You can use these any time of the class or semester to capture a level of how students feel about class. Our friends in the field tell us that we must use a Likert Scale for attitudinal capture, which means for psychometric purposes you have five levels of satisfaction (5=Extremely Satisfied, 4=Somewhat Satisfied, 3=Neutral, 2=Somewhat Dissatisfied, and 1=Completely and Utterly Dissatisfied with this Waste of Time). On a questionnaire for students about their in-class use of portable electronic devices (PEDS— we just made up the acronym because educational researchers love to do it, and it's quite easy), you could ask about actual usage (where 5 = "I'm on my PED 100% of class time" and 1 = "I dread my PED").
- **Finish the article.** You could have a results section, a discussion section, and even future directions section.
- **Submit the article.** If you're not sure where, check out the appendices in *Enhancing Scholarly Work on Teaching & Learning*. At the end Maryellen Weimer has an appendix on Discipline-Based Pedagogical Periodicals and another on Cross-Disciplinary and Topical Pedagogical Periodicals. Gain the experience of actual submission.
- **Alternatively, you might try our aforementioned market research plan.** Read through some of the journals that accept SOTL and analyze one that seems appealing to you. For instance, the aforementioned Maryellen Weimer is editor of *The Teaching Professor* that publishes such articles. Her preferred article length is much shorter than that of some other journals. Try picking one of these journals and targeting your article towards its preferences.

- **Think of the rejection slip as a mentoring process.** We hope that your very first try gets accepted, but if it doesn't, don't despair. Most journals now use a peer-review process with two or three reviewers. If your piece is rejected, most editors send along the anonymous reviewers' comments on your work. Study them carefully. Some of the comments and standards you might be tempted to reject, but if you resubmit, you are going to have to satisfy the same folks. Some rejections are conditional; if you are willing to make some changes, the editor may publish your work. We were honed on the popular fiction market where editors always made some changes (perhaps it's an ego thing), so we have no trouble accepting their advice, especially since we're strange scholars in a strange land.
- **Do it again.** As Roethke says, I learn by going where I have to go.

Hal Blythe
Charlie Sweet
Eastern Kentucky University

Blending Service into Scholarship

Teaching + Scholarship + Service = the "traditional" 3-legged stool used by non-tenured faculty to navigate through the tenure landmines and subsequently continue to be labeled "productive." A "modified" model encourages these energetic researchers to embrace the scholarship of teaching, thus, writing about unique teaching methods or interesting case studies used in the classroom. My proposed model bends the traditional model even further and encourages scholarship of service.

Typically, faculty are assigned/volunteered/or thrust onto a committee/task force/project because they missed the meeting and got voted onto the group, because it looks good on the P&T document, or because no one else would agree to do this project ... unless he/she had the least seniority and needed the brownie points. I suggest instead to embrace the opportunity to volunteer/be assigned/be thrust into a service project and transform the perceived drudgery of the service project into a robust research agenda.

Proposed Scholarship of Service Model
- Does the process to complete the service project present an interesting/unique research idea?
- If it does, before you begin the project, design your scholarly-based research methodology to capture the process and publish an article which highlights your project design, research methods, and process.

- Does the service project present an interesting/unique research idea?
- If it does, before you begin the project, design your scholarly-based literature review to explain the rationale behind completing the service project and publish an article which highlights the project, literature review, and the worth of the project.

Methodology for Utilizing the Scholarship of Service Model
"Assigned" service = scholarship

Assigned to teach the dreaded freshman orientation class? Turn this into a scholarly exercise by surveying the freshman as to what topics were helpful in their acclimation into college life. Further enhance your research by following up with the cohort groups two years later to look at the same question of "helpfulness" and retention. End result for this author = 2 journal publications. End result for the institution = modifications to the freshman orientation curriculum as well as providing vital data used to enhance university retention efforts.

"Thrust" service = scholarship

Thrust into helping out with a service project before you can run away? Just cannot say "no" when a colleague realizes that the institution needs a disruptive student policy? Turn this type of service into scholarship by surveying similar colleges to determine the definitions of disruptive behavior. Using the gathered quantitative and qualitative data, actually write the policy which administrators and faculty alike will support due to the research-based method of defining the terminology. Turn this data gathering into scholarship by explaining the method of data collection, detailing how the policy was developed and adopted, and even writing about the training developed to implement the policy. End result for this author = 1 journal publication, 2 conference proceedings, 3 magazine publications. End result for the institution = disruptive student policy that benefitted not only the institution but also was widely disseminated to other institutions.

"Volunteer" service = scholarship

Imagine just walking down the hall and your Associate Dean casually remarks, "Wouldn't it be a great idea if we had a week during the semester to encourage our students to focus on and discuss ethics and social responsibility?" Of course it is a great idea for the students, and it is a great opportunity for you to volunteer to coordinate an ethics awareness week.

- Suggestion – start small – one or two activities in a week; eight years later and four ethic awareness weeks – be ready to have your research agenda consumed by this service project.
- Develop a theme for the week – resulting in scholarship utilizing student-led research about a particular theme/idea as well as case study publications.

- Develop a method for assessing ethics that results in scholarship describing the assessment method and reporting on the results.
- Develop a project that encourages students to volunteer and report on the results of their volunteer projects on posters – resulting in scholarship highlighting extensive literature review focusing on reasons for volunteering coupled with possibility of a longitudinal study.

End result for this author = 4 journal publications, 1 case study, 7 conference proceedings, 1 magazine publication. End result for the institution = 4 completed ethics awareness weeks (offered every 2 years) which provide ethics assessment for accreditation purposes as well as an opportunity for approximately 1,000 students each time to pause and consider varying issues dealing with ethics and social responsibility.

Suggestions for aspiring researchers

Approach a service project with a positive perspective – is there anything about this project that could be improved; could the project be adapted and explained so that other institutions might benefit from your mistakes/lessons learned; will this project be met with such resistance from faculty/administration that being able to state that the definitions/policy/process is based upon a research agenda might soften the introduction of the idea or project; or is it just such an interesting project that perhaps it can be a case study?

The key is pre-planning. Approach each service opportunity with a research-based mindset and determine if there is any possible scholarly output from this activity. If so, from the outset of the service project, plan to seamlessly incorporate your research methods into the process, the project, and the outcome. Not surprisingly, using this Scholarship of Service Model will not only enhance your research agenda, but also it will raise the quality of the service project.

So, next time you are late to a meeting and for "punishment" your fellow faculty members elect you to organize the annual student recruitment fair, pause for a few moments and ponder, could this be my next journal article about ....

Judy Spain
Eastern Kentucky University

Publishing Ideas from Courses that Extend Beyond Your Primary Discipline

When I teach courses that push me outside of my "primary" mathematics boundaries, I look for opportunities to present my experiences in presentations and articles. In particular, I have taught a course entitled Analytics for my university's Honors Program and another course entitled Living With Limitations that is a part of our First-Year Seminar course offerings. Most recently I have taught my Introduction to Mathematical Reasoning course as part of a linked cohort with an Introduction to Psychological Science course. After teaching a course of this nature (namely, one that pushes me outside my typical mathematics framework), I initially seek venues where I can give a presentation about the experience. I've been able to give such presentations at mathematics meetings (regional or national meetings of the Mathematical Association of America, in particular) and teaching/learning conferences (for example, the Lilly Conference on College Teaching at Miami University in Oxford, Ohio).

For the Analytics course, which fulfills the mathematics general education requirement for our Honors Program students, I combine with the core mathematical ideas some topics from philosophy of science, basic ideas of computer logic, and general notions of critical thinking. The mathematical content includes problem solving, symbolic logic, counting, voting methods, graph theory and recursive functions. After offering several presentations about the course at a variety of mathematics and teaching/learning conferences, I was invited to submit a paper based on the presentations. At that point, the paper was not difficult to pull together from the presentations. The resulting publication is listed in the references at the end of this tip [2].

My university's First-Year Seminar (FYS) course is required of all freshman, with "ways of knowing" as the broad theme for all instructors who develop and teach an FYS course. My FYS course, entitled Living With Limitations, is framed around various limits that we encounter; these limits include disabilities of any kind and identity issues. The course is far from being a mathematics course; however, I have found a variety of ways to incorporate some basic quantitative reasoning components into the course, both in connection with the broad ways of knowing theme and my more specific focus on limitations. Consequently, I developed a presentation or two about the course for mathematics and teaching/learning meetings. Once again, after presenting the course at a mathematics session, I was invited to submit a paper that further developed the ideas of my presentation. See the list of references for the paper that was eventually published [1].

Freshmen and sophomores on our campus are required, as part of their general education, to take a pair of courses together that are referred to as linked cohort courses

(LCC). In my case, I paired my Introduction to Mathematical Reasoning general education course with an Introduction to Psychological Science course. The same group of students took both LCC courses in the given semester. The Psychology course instructor and I were challenged to build mathematics/psychology connections for the students. As this course has just ended, I haven't yet been able to develop a presentation or write an article about the experience. However, following my previous roadmap for scholarly publications, I plan to develop presentations for both mathematics and teaching/learning conferences. Hopefully that will lead to an opportunity to submit an article to a peer-reviewed scholarly research journal.

Teaching courses like the ones I've described above has provided me with some good ways to be innovative as a teacher and to be rejuvenated during my teaching career. By connecting these rich teaching experiences with scholarship, I have been able to integrate two components of my professional life as a faculty member at an institution that emphasizes excellent teaching.

References

1. Pinter, Mike. "Some Mathematical Elements in a First-Year Seminar Course", *PRIMUS: Problems, Resources, and Issues in Mathematics Undergraduate Studies*, Volume 17, Issue 1, March 2007, pp. 44-51.
2. Pinter, Mike. "Analytics: An Integrated Mathematics, Logic and Philosophy of Science Course" – in *Selected Papers from the Eleventh International Conference on College Teaching and Learning* (2000).

Mike Pinter
Belmont University

S-t-r-e-t-c-h-i-n-g Yourself: Writing Outside Your Comfort Zone

Familiarity can be comfortable and reassuring, but familiarity can also breed contempt. What else can be said about a topic about which you've written/presented for several years? If you haven't completely exhausted all there is to be said by you about the topic, try a new venue. If you always seek publication in trade journals, such as English-language journals, go broader to include language-arts journals (or vice versa). Feel as though there's nothing left to say about your topic? Take a new angle that necessitates your going back to the literature. Better yet, try a new topic, whether related or completely different. Novelty will certainly require you to think in a new way and to use some forethought, but may also inspire your creative muse and make the writing process exciting again.

Leslie Elrod
University of Cincinnati RWC

Young Adult Literature as a Publishing Venure for the Higher Education Scholar

In a *New Yorker* cartoon from the 1990's, a pack of wolves are baying at the moon. One wolf at the back of the group turns to another and asks, "Do you think we're having an impact?" The same question might be asked among academics in terms of their scholarship — "are we having an impact?" To all but a few best-selling university scholars, the consumers of our research are often few and the "impact" limited.

Ray Granastein in his book *Who Killed Canadian History?* has painted a bleak picture of academic publishing. "The standard university press run for most specialized academic history books is now about 400-800 copies, usually tending toward the lower end," he writes.

Granastein reports that royalties, if they are paid at all, are in the range of 1-5 percent of the net price, compared with 10-15 percent of the list price paid by trade publishers. Adding to this already gloomy scene, some presses require a printing fee or require the author to turn in a "print-ready" file saving the publisher the cost of doing the typesetting.

Adding to the already troubling situation, the price of academic books is inevitably high – usually above $40. (In a listing of recently published books in *The Chronicle of Higher Education* a few titles were marked as high as $75-$95.) Granastein says that "Often their only destination is university libraries and even specialists no longer buy the books published by their peers; certainly the public does not purchase them."

The publishing scene can indeed be discouraging. The market includes tough facts such as there are 500,000 new books produced each year, which is about 10,000 books per week. The return rate is 40%, which means barely a majority of all books written are "making it." Those that get noticed are even fewer. The *Washington Post Book World* evaluates 150 select books each week and reviews about 15. The *New York Times Book Review* will publish about 20 to 25 each week. A recent panel of writers on C-SPAN's "Book TV" noted that book reviewing in general has become a lost art with fewer appearing in outlets. (On a more positive note, the Internet has become an increasingly popular location for book reviews.)

In this environment, what can academics do to reach a wider audience with their work? One possible answer for educators, educational historians and biographers, and professional educators is the arena of young adult books. First, some definitions. Author and publishing advisor Aaron Shepherd labels middle school nonfiction trade books as including grades 4 to 6, 60 to 100 pages in length, and usually published in slightly oversized paperback format. Young adult nonfiction trade books are written for grades 7 and up, are usually 100 to 150 pages long, and published in standard paperback or hardback format. So why should an academic turn to this venue?

A personal vignette. I published, with a strong academic press, *And There Were Giants in the Land: The Life of William Heard Kilpatrick*. Kilpatrick was a well-known disciple of John Dewey in the first half of the twentieth century and an influential progressive educator. The book was 500 pages in length, contained 1200 footnotes, and was a Critics Choice selection by the American Educational Studies Association. The work received 10 positive reviews of 11 in the literature, including one from the *Harvard Educational Review*. Since then, its publication has been referenced multiple times in other scholarly works. In other words, it was a scholarly work that had an above average acceptance by the academic community.

I next came across a subject and story that I thought worthy of a book-length treatment and decided to use the young adult book format. It was the narrative of my public school teacher and coach who broke the color line in athletics, education, law enforcement, and politics. Playing off the subject's track and field specialty, the high hurdles, I titled the book *Going Over All the Hurdles: A Life of Oatess Archey*. I found a publisher in a state historical society press's young adult biographical series. In *six months* I sold more copies of the young adult book than I sold of the scholarly book in *ten years*. Back to our cartoon wolves and the question of impact. In one year I gave talks to over

600 students; undertook in-service presentations to librarians, teachers, and teacher education students; spoke at book signings; and presented at state historical meetings. The book also received an award by a university and public library organization in addition to being a finalist for two national book prizes.

Why don't academics write young adult books? First and foremost, such books may not count toward tenure or be viewed as scholarly. Others may not be familiar with the genre and know how to go about it. Or there may be no interest or time to devote to such a project. And for some, young adult books may seem like mere popularizing.

Then what are some reasons that academics should become involved in this genre? To begin, the authorship of many young adult books is left to individuals who may or may not be specialists. To use history as an example, James Loewen, author of the provocatively titled book, *Lies My Teacher Told Me: Everything Your American History Textbook Got Wrong*, claims that it is editorial staffs at publishing houses writing or having a major influence over the textbooks and trade books they produce. Loewen reports that some texts, especially at the middle school and high school level, once had historians doing all the writing, but that is not occurring much anymore. High school history texts are now written by a mix of historians, social studies educators, multicultural specialists, and curriculum professors. So, for example, who's writing young adult biographies? A random search of my own institution's collection and the collection of our public library indicated few if any are historians or educators – they are writers (authors).

Let me quickly say that this is not to denigrate outstanding authors who write in the arena of young adult literature. There are many outstanding authors producing solid works in history and other areas. Russell Freedman, for example, has written stellar works in history and biography. Freedman has written that "the best way to introduce yourself to a new subject is pick up a children's book." His works on Babe Didrikson Zaharias, Eleanor Roosevelt, and Abraham Lincoln are models for any scholar writing in the biographical arena.

But what can academics add? Why should historians or professional educators write young adult books? First, they have expertise in their field and know how to go about research. David McCullough, historian and bestselling author, has written that "In the writing of history and biography, one has to call on imagination — in the sense of transporting oneself into that other time and the lives of those people, all but vanished, distant, and different. That takes research and analysis to be sure." In a young adult book I recently read, the author, in a short bibliographic essay, indicated how a primary source (a set of letters) started her on the way to writing the book. To her it seemed a discovery. For historians primary sources are familiar tools of the trade.

Another reason that academics should write young adult books is that they are usually good writers. They have spent years writing as part of their professional preparation. And, if an academic has spent part of his/her career teaching in a K-12 classroom, he/she knows students and what students like to read. Gay Ivey, writing in the journal

Educational Leadership, has said, "You can't learn much from books that don't matter to you. The right books can help students care about content." She added, "Instead of focusing on how to get students to <u>remember</u> what they read, our best bet is to provide texts that are more <u>memorable</u>."

Popularization can also be a stigma for academics keeping them away from young adult literature. As a junior high student I began reading the books of the bestselling author Thomas B. Costain. Although he did write three young adult books, he was mainly known for his historical novels. (He also wrote a number of historical works on Canada and England.) All of his books were meticulously researched, engaging, and extremely well written. And I would have to say that my interest in history can be attributed to the work of Costain. Being popular and being a scholar are not mutually exclusive.

What are some good topics for young adult books? The fields of social studies, language arts, science, and the arts are all critical and desirable areas. In other words — non-fiction. In three research studies, young adult book author Denise Johnson found that when children and young adults were given a choice of books to read, nonfiction was their preference. (The National Endowment for the Arts reported in 2007 that fiction reading had declined sharply among younger readers.) Yet studies have shown a dearth of nonfiction books for young readers due to limited exposure of these books by teachers, the dominance in schools of basal readers, the limited selection and availability of these books, and a lack of teacher knowledge on how to teach from nonfiction trade books. *Writer's Digest* (special issue "Writer's Yearbook 2010") has reported "The young adult (YA) book sector remained strong (in a challenging economic year), partly because more adults were starting to read YA titles. Children's/YA hardcover sales were up 30.7% the first half of 2009 compared to adult hardcover decrease of 17.8%."

Biographies, which can cover most if not all of the above fields of study, is an excellent genre for young adult books. Author Tracy Dils has written that biographies are one of the most popular nonfiction categories. Most of the winners of the Carter G. Woodson Book Award — a prize given to social studies trade books — are biographies. While biographies can be about famous individuals, young adults like to read about young adults – and if the book is about a life, material on the subject's childhood and young adult period should be prominently included. Denise Johnson has given four categories of biographical subjects: 1) Discovery and Exploration, 2) Political Leaders and Social Activists, 3) Artists and Authors, and 4) People Who Have Persevered.

What are possible publishing venues for young adult literature? They include:
- State or provincial historical presses
- University presses (highly selective)
- Specialty presses (see writing magazines and books or Google by topic)
- Faith-based presses
- Regional publishers – e.g. Midwest, New England, the South

- Topical presses that focus, for example, on gender, ethnicity, physical fitness/sports, or the environment

Young adult books may not be the right fit for all academics. But higher education scholars can contribute much to work of our K-12 schools. The editors of *Teaching U.S. History: Dialogues among Social Studies Teachers and Historians* have written this about history professors: "It is time for historians to stop merely complaining about how poorly prepared college freshmen are in history and to work to address this problem by helping to enrich the historical teaching enterprise in the earlier grade levels." Academic scholars can find a viable, appropriate, and often little-used platform for their research and be able to answer in the affirmative the question posed by our *New Yorker* wolf — "are we having an impact?"

John Beineke
Arkansas State University

Sustaining Scholarship in a Digital Era

With the number of peer-reviewed online journals increasing, faculty members will continue to find themselves immersed in a culture of digital scholarship. Kristine L. Blair, Gail E. Hawisher, and Cynthia L. Selfe highlight the importance of remaining relevant in a changing electronic landscape. While they discuss electronic journal editing specifically, I use this example as an entry point into a larger conversation taking place in the academy, highlighting the importance of redefining the scholar in a digitally defined era.

Within composition, several online peer-reviewed journals have experienced success, including *Kairos, Praxis, Rhizomes,* and *Computers and Composition Online*. Prominent national conferences, such as Computers and Writing, have sustained their face-to-face meetings and expanded to offer online sessions as well (Computers and Writing Online). Scholars like Cheryl Ball have developed fully online digital tenure portfolios. The academic terrain is changing. While books and print-centric media will continue to hold a significant presence in academic communities, scholars must be responsive to 21st-century literacies as well. What does this mean for sustaining scholarship?

As Ernest L. Boyer suggests, "Alternating periods of goal-seeking and reassessment should be common for all academics" (48). Sustainable scholars might become not only active consumers of digital information, including scholarly databases, listservs, blogs, and wikis; they should also play a role in shaping the content. Scholarly sustainability means learning new literacies, composing in virtual spaces, and producing information, even scholarship, in digital environments.

As a scholar interested in exploring new opportunities in my field, this meant proposing traditional conference papers for presentation in synchronous online venues. Parts of the process were similar. I received a CFP from a national organization, wrote a conference proposal based on the theme and my current scholarship in the area, and then later received acceptance to attend the event and present the conference paper. The major difference was not the peer-review process or the rigor of the traditional selection process but the way in which the paper was delivered. It was online; therefore, I challenged myself to try a new medium to broaden opportunities for scholarship. Surprisingly, I found that I grew more as a scholar by exploring this event than I had in years of traditional face-to-face conferences. What does this mean for sustaining scholarship? Explore venues for scholarly growth, which might mean taking the time to pursue intellectual opportunities in new mediums.

Acquisition of and access to digital literacies should be a collective interest for scholars. These literacies pose new challenges while offering scholarly venues for exploration and experimentation. Sustainable scholars will seize opportunities to exploit new literacy practices. These developments invite scholars to reconsider their intellectual practices and potentially expand notions of creating, composing, and researching. An interest in digital spaces does not mean relearning or changing what we research; moreover, it provides opportunities to explore new realms and scholarly platforms. At least, that is the claim that I make here. Sustainability in a digital era provides an opportunity for expanded notions of scholarship for those willing to accept this new challenge.

References

Ball, Cheryl. "About this Portfolio." Retrieved June 10, 2010, from <http://www.ceball.com/tenure/welcome-to-my-portfolio/about/>.

Blair, Kristine L., Gail E. Hawisher, and Cynthia L. Selfe. "*The Electronic Landscape of Journal Editing:* Computers and Composition *as a Scholarly Collective.*" *Profession 2009.* Ed. Rosemary G. Feal. New Work: Modern Language Association, 2009. Print.

Boyer, Ernest L. *Scholarship Reconsidered: Priorities of the Professoriate.* Princeton, NJ: Carnegie Foundation for the Advancement of Teaching, 1990. Print.

Computers and Writing Online. Retrieved June 10, 2010, from <http://www.digitalparlor.org/cw2010/>.

Rusty Carpenter
Eastern Kentucky University

Presenting Live in South Africa... from My Family Room

Not so long ago the idea of presenting at a conference via distance technologies was daunting. One had to hope to arrange for special rooms equipped with expensive high-end video and audio capabilities – on both ends of the conversation. Such rooms are rare in many parts of the world, so it was a special treat when I was able to present at an international conference live in the Republic of South Africa ... from my family room. The hardest part was figuring out what time I had to be ready, to match the gathering taking place 8,454 miles away.

The opportunity began typically enough. Attorney Paul Colditz, the president of South Africa's association of governing boards (equivalent to the National School Boards Association in America) was interested in learning more about the landmark Kentucky case, Rose *v Council for Better Education*, the topic of my dissertation. He travelled to the University of Kentucky for a legal seminar, and to learn more about the case when Dr. Lars Bjork , a mutual colleague of ours who chairs the Department of Educational Leadership at the University of Kentucky (UK), invited us both to dinner to discuss the case. After the meeting, Colditz invited me to present at the 6th International Symposium on School Reform in July, 2010, near Pretoria, South Africa.

But there was a problem. Money.

Being in my first-year as a tenure-track faculty member at Eastern Kentucky University, I lacked the resources for the $2,000 airfare and other expenses required to make a presentation possible. Despite the personal benefit I might derive from adding a prestigious item to my vitae, I was forced to decline the invitation. But in doing so, I wondered aloud to Dr. Bjork about the possibility of using high-speed internet technologies for such an event.

Bjork gave this some thought and turned to another UK colleague, Dr. Justin Bathon, for his expertise. Bathon devised a simple solution that combined a few readily available technologies that were capable of producing an end-user experience that very closely matched what academic conference attendees have come to expect.

On July 20th, at 12:30 PM South Africa time, approximately 40 participants at the ISER conference filed into a meeting room. Before them was Mr. Colditz and Dr. Bjork, who facilitated the session. After introductory remarks, I appeared on the screen in the conference room and made my presentation. I decided to go "old school," using notes but no PowerPoint slides. That was immediately followed by the traditional question and answer session. Again I appeared on the screen, but this time I was wearing a different shirt and tie, it was 6:30 AM eastern time, and I was in my family room at home. The only difference for the audience was that when scholars wanted to ask a question, they walked to the front of the room, where their voice and image was picked up by the laptop computer positioned there.

Here's how we did it.

About two weeks before the conference, I went to UK and met with Bathon to record my presentation. Using a Flip Video Camera on a simple tripod, Bathon shot my presentation. Bathon then took the video and edited it, adding two or three title slides. He saved the video in two forms, one high-quality for the presentation, and another lower quality that would work well on the blogs that both Bathon and I write. The high quality video was recorded on DVD and sent to South Africa. Recording the high-quality video on DVD had a second advantage. It would not need time to load up on a computer while participants were waiting, thus making a better experience for the attendees.

My choice of presenting as a "talking head" required some additional support for the audience. For that reason, notes for the presentation were sent in advance to Dr. Johan Beckman, Chair of the Educational Leadership and Policy Department at the University of Pretoria, for posting on his blog, which made them available to all conference attendees. I was also able to provide links to additional resources related to my presentation.

When the question and answer session began, we switched technologies, using Skype for interactive video conferencing. I had never used Skype before (available at skype.com), but found it to be simple and effective. I had to load the free software on my computer and buy a webcam. I was advised that virtually all webcams priced above $50 were probably of sufficient quality, but I opted for an $80 Logitech 2-megapixel autofocus webcam that was easy to set up and performed very well.

A similar setup, using Skype and a webcam, was installed on the computer belonging to School of Achievement Principal, Tinus Du Preez, who assisted Dr. Bjork in the South African meeting room. Prior to the conference, Mr. Du Preez and I tested our connections a couple of times to make sure we knew how Skype functioned and that we had our time zones correct. It turns out that Skype helped us with that too by posting the actual time of day for the location one is speaking to in an information bar at the top of the Skype screen.

So by that means, I was able to gain an international presentation credit from my family room. I will follow that up with a formal paper that will be part of the conference proceedings.

Instead of spending $3,000 to attend the conference I spent $80 for a webcam, a fortunate circumstance in tight budgetary times. And, I now have a video and notes that I can use in class. While it may not be practical for everyone to present in this way, it worked for me as a scholar-teacher.

Richard Day
Eastern Kentucky University

Merging Discipline-Based Scholarship with the Scholarship of Teaching

Before outlining this tip, let us start with a **disclaimer**: this tip is ONLY for those individuals who are at an academic institution or teaching within an academic department that would recognize scholarship of teaching and learning work and publications in the merit and promotion and tenure processes.

It has been our experience as we each have mentored tenure-track faculty in our departments and assisted them in making progress toward promotion and tenure that many come in with the notion that teaching and scholarship are – indeed, must be – completely separate. We do not concur. We believe teaching can inform scholarship and scholarship can inform teaching.

As a psychologist and a political scientist, our disciplines involve –at the core – people. As such, it is easy to make the argument that the research we do in the classroom could inform what we do in the lab or vice versa. But, we do not believe this merging of teaching and scholarship is restricted to persons in the social sciences. Consider a colleague in Math, for example. He was having difficulty deciding on an area of scholarship. One of us (RO) encouraged him to consider what elements of his teaching might link to scholarship in Math. With some guidance from us, he decided that one of the primary road blocks to his effectively teaching Math was math phobia. We assisted him in developing a service learning project that involved students in the math course tutoring students in basic math in elementary school. He was able to show that this service-learning experience lowered the college students' math anxiety (employing a pre-post measure of math anxiety) and that these decreases in math anxiety were positively related to improved performance in the math course. Granted, this is not math scholarship that has generated a new formula or some new calculation – but is it not relevant to both the discipline and his role as a teacher?

We both have spent many years doing research – separately – on psychological and political correlates of racial prejudice and hatred. We developed hypotheses about how elements of critical thinking could be employed to reduce prejudice and hatred. But how could we test these assumptions? We believe we can (and have) test(ed) these assumptions by merging our scholarship and our teaching. We developed a team-taught course on the Politics and Psychology of Hatred, outlined this critical thinking model as an essential element of the course, and have gathered data (and published articles and book chapters!) over the years addressing how these patterns of critical thinking can be taught, nurtured, facilitated and enhanced. At the same time, we have gathered evidence that enhancing these skills results in a reduction in prejudicial attitudes and hate-based behavior. We believe that this merging of our scholarship and our teaching has allowed us to study topics that, otherwise, would have remained too "big picture" to have been studied. This merging has increased our scholarly productivity and efficiency immensely.

Some readers may be thinking – "Well, I don't have the luxury of team-teaching a class or developing special topics courses like the kind that you described." That's fine. There are other examples. Let us say you are teaching Social Psychology. An important topic in that course is "interpersonal relationships." Think about what skills might be related to effectiveness in interpersonal relationships. Think about what teaching strategies and activities you could design for your course that might enhance these skills. One could gather data before and after employing teaching activities and strategies designed to promote growth in interpersonal skills and explore the relationship between use of these techniques and some measure of improved success in interpersonal relationships.

Or, using political science as an example, imagine that you are teaching a course in Political Theory. Perhaps you believe that a firm understanding of political theory is essential for motivating students to become more civically engaged. Surely, as a political scientist, one's department would see the value in enhancing students' civic-engagement. Or, let us use a non-social science discipline. Imagine that you teach literature. You believe that students do not have enough "appreciation" of literature. Perhaps a service-learning experience for a literature course could be developed where students are required to go out into the community and read to underprivileged youth. One could assess the impact of such an experience on student perceptions of the importance of literature.

The point is simply this – discipline-based research and teaching can be merged in such a way as to enhance one's effectiveness as a teacher-scholar. By merging one's discipline-based scholarship with one's teaching, both are enhanced and one's publishing opportunities are likely doubled. One can submit such work to publishing venues such as the current line of publications (It Works For Me!), discipline-based scholarship journals (such as *Social Justice Research*), discipline-based teaching journals (such as *Teaching of Psychology* or *Teaching Political Science*), journals on the scholarship of teaching and learning (such as *Journal on Excellence in College Teaching*), or (depending on what format one is using to deliver the course) journals that are devoted to promoting excellence in different formats for teaching (such as *Journal of Online Teaching and Learning*), or journals devoted to promoting excellence with various teaching tools (such as *Journal of Educational Computing Research*).

Randall Osborne
Texas State U.–San Marcos
Paul Kriese
Indiana University East